BLACK DOG OPERA LIBRARY

The Barber of Seville

The Barber of Seville

GIOACCHINO ROSSINI

TEXT BY DAVID FOIL

BLACK DOG
& LEVENTHAL
PUBLISHERS
NEW YORK

Published by
Black Dog & Leventhal Publishers, Inc.
151 West 19th Street
New York, NY 10011

Distributed by
Workman Publishing Company
708 Broadway
New York, NY 10003

Designed by Alleycat Design, Inc.

Series editor: Jessica MacMurray

Photo Research: Diana Gongora

Book manufactured in Singapore

ISBN: 1-57912-020-2

h g f e d c

FOREWORD

The Barber of Seville is perhaps the most important and influential comedic opera in the modern repertoire. It is truly a masterpiece—for its composer and its genre in terms of structure, form and content. But, at the same time, it can only be so because it is so full of exciting, fun, beautiful music. An *opera buffa* in the classic sense, *The Barber of Seville* is dynamic without being confusing, funny without being preposterous, touching without being melodramatic and full of some of the most fantastic music in nineteenth century opera.

Explore the pages of this book: learn about the origins of the operas, the lives of the composers, and the world of opera singers and conductors. Listen to the complete opera on the two CD's included in the inside front and back covers of this book, while following along with the complete libretto. You will find both an English and an Italian version, complete with annotations by the author.

Enjoy this book and enjoy the music.

ABOUT THE AUTHOR

David Foil is the author of the six-volume Black Dog Music Library and the first four volumes of the Black Dog Opera Library. A native of Louisiana, he has written extensively about music, theater and film, both as a critic for newspapers in the South and as an annotator for a wide range of classical recordings for the Angel/EMI classics, Columbia and Sony Classical labels. He lives in New York City.

GIOACCHINO ROSSINI (1792-1868).

The Barber of Seville

When he was an old man, the Jupiter of Italian opera, Giuseppe Verdi, was moved to write to a friend, "I confess that I cannot help believing *Il Barbiere di Siviglia,* for abundance of ideas, for comic verve, and for truth of declamation, the most beautiful *opera buffa* in existence." Since Verdi was not given to hyperbole, his words spin and dazzle like the greatest compliment in the history of music. Verdi knew what he was talking about: when he wrote these words in 1898, he had already composed his miraculous, quicksilver *Falstaff,* as perfect and elegant a comic opera as one can imagine. But *Falstaff* was a different kind of comedy, like Mozart's *The Marriage of Figaro* and Wagner's *Die Meistersinger von Nürnberg*—a human comedy, just a heartbeat away from tragedy, its radiant humor and high spirits streaked with shadow and melancholy. *Opera buffa* is another matter, silly, giddy and uproarious by comparison. And, as Verdi suggested, there is no argument that Giaocchino Rossini's *Il Barbiere di Siviglia* is its ideal.

The Italian word *buffa* means "puff" or "gust." When it is used to describe an opera, it suggests the kind of breathless comedy we might call madcap, screwball, or slapstick—maybe all three, at once. Think of a Marx Brothers movie, one of the *Pink Panther* series with Peter Sellers, or a memorable episode of *I Love Lucy;* that is buffa comedy. Rossini wrote in this style better and more consistently than any other composer. He wrote other inspired buffa comedies, such as *La Cenerentola, L'Italiana in Algeri, Il Turco in Italia, Il Viaggio a Reims* and *Le Comte Ory.* But none of them sparkles and delights quite like *Il Barbiere di Siviglia* (which we'll now refer to as *The Barber of Seville).*

Part of the charm is the story itself. It is drawn from the hugely popular stage comedy of the same name by the French playwright Beaumarchais (1732-99), a man whose fortunes rose and fell repeatedly as a financial speculator,

P. A. CARON DE BEAUMARCHAIS.

secret agent, gun-runner and man of letters who even had a significant hand in French involvement in the American Revolution. At least as fascinating as his own characters, Beaumarchais (whose real name was Pierre Augustin Caron) wrote a trilogy of deftly satirical comedies that followed the relationships of a group of characters from both the servant class and the nobility—*Le Barbier de Seville, Le Mariage de Figaro* and *La Mère coupable.* In pre-Revolutionary Paris, the political impact of the first two plays was considerable. The

PIERRE AUGUSTE CARON DE BEAUMARCHAIS
(1732-1799)

character of Figaro, the barber of Seville who gets married in its sequel, is a gifted and wily man (not unlike Beaumarchais) who is passionate about the idea of personal freedom and individual dignity. But he is trapped in a society where a man like his master, Count Almaviva, always has the upper hand. The buoyant *Le Barbier de Seville* was a stage triumph in Paris in 1775. Six years later, though, Louis XVI was so offended by the impertinence of the more critical *Le Mariage de Figaro* that he banned it outright, and it was not performed for several years.

Beaumarchais' first play tells how the resourceful Figaro helps Count Almaviva win the hand of the beautiful Rosina, who becomes the Countess in the second play. The playwright planned *Le Barbier de Seville* as a comic opera, possibly using songs he had collected during a visit to Spain. His libretto was rejected by the Opéra Comique in Paris. An operatic version did emerge, though, in St. Petersburg in 1782, written by the Italian composer Giovanni Paisiello, who was then Catherine the Great's music master. Paisiello's *Il Barbiere di Siviglia* was a great success and became a staple of the European repertoire of comic operas. (Mozart's opera of *Le Mariage de Figaro,* in Italian, followed in 1786.) When Rossini approached the idea of writing his own opera of *Le Barbier de Seville* in 1816, the popularity of Paisiello's version concerned him, and some accounts suggest that he sought Paisiello's blessing.

But there was no copyright law at the time, and the popular play was fair game. In addition to the Paisiello, there were no less than five other operatic versions of Beaumarchais' play written between its premiere and the first performance of Rossini's opera. The libretto for Rossini's *The Barber of Seville,* by Cesare Sterbini, is a shrewd adaptation of the play (with a fair amount of borrowing from Paisiello's libretto) that emphasizes the story's screwball elements, not its political satire. It is a fine framework for a comic opera. But the genius

GIOVANNI PAISELLO (1740-1816), WHO WROTE ANOTHER POPULAR VERSION OF *BARBER* BEFORE ROSSINI'S MASTERPIECE WAS COMPOSED.

in The Barber of Seville is Rossini's. Inspired by his libretto, the composer provided music that never fails to disarm and delight, almost two centuries later. The score is inexhaustibly tuneful, deft and magical in its expressive skill, and as sensuous and effervescent as a fine Champagne. Most of all, it sparkles with Rossini's inimitable musical wit. He was a fine composer of dramatic operas, but his sense of comedy was incomparable. No other composer could make music laugh and smile so winningly, not even Mozart.

And here is the most amazing fact: Rossini did it all in less than a month. *The Barber of Seville* had its premiere in Rome on February 20, 1816, at the Teatro Argentina during the Carnival season. By all accounts, the 22-year-old Rossini did not even receive the libretto to begin work until the last week of January. He had started the 1815-16 season in Naples, where he was under contract to direct the theaters and compose a number of new operas for the season. The first of them was the serious opera *Elisabetta, Regina d'Inghilterra* (Elizabeth, Queen of England), which had its premiere on October 4 at the city's Teatro SanCarlo. Rossini's Neopolitan contract allowed him some freedom, though. He took advantage of it to accept an invitation to spend the late fall and early winter in Rome. In addition to writing another serious opera, *Torvaldo e Dorliska,* and supervising a new production of his *Il Turco in Italia* at the Teatro Valle in November and December, he agreed to write a pair of lighter works for the pre-Lenten Carnival season that followed, under the patronage of the Duke of Sforza-Cesarini, who owned and operated the Teatro Argentina.

All of this sounds grand and a bit glamorous in retrospect; in reality, it proved to be an ordeal verging on catastrophe. Control of Rome had just been returned to the Vatican, with the collapse of the Napoleonic Empire. Papal authorities chose to administer the city's theaters with an iron and censorious hand, slashing the subsidy granted them by the Napoleonic government. While audiences loved *Il Turco in Italia, Torvaldo e Dorliska* was a fiasco in its premiere on December 26, 1815. Rossini was probably glad to have the Teatro Argentina commission to follow it. But the situation that greeted him was dire. To make ends meet there, the Duke was forced to plan a crowd-pleasing season of comic opera. He had such a difficult time gathering his ensemble that he was forced to stage Rossini's *L'Italiana in Algeri*—already old hat, having been written two-and-a-half years earlier—in order to open by mid-January. The conditions were gruelling. Contemporary accounts reveal that the Teatro Argentina was a dingy, filthy and uncomfortable place, typical of Roman theaters of the day. To get *L'Italiana in Algeri* on its feet, Rossini and his singers endured agonizing rehearsals in unheated rooms in the damp chill of the Roman winter. As if the situation were not grim enough already, the utterly exhausted 44-year-old Duke of Sforza-Cesarini died suddenly of a stroke in the early morning hours of February 7, 1816, the day after Rossini delivered the completed score for Act I of his new comic opera. It was in this atmosphere of seething tension, personal discomfort, budgetary nightmares and sudden death that he wrote *The Barber of Seville.*

Or what became *The Barber of Seville*. When the opera had its premiere, it was entitled *Almaviva o sia L'Inutile Precauzione* (Almaviva, or The Futile Precaution), perhaps because of Rossini's fear of offending Paisiello and the fans of his opera. (Almost 60 years later, Verdi would similarly wonder whether he should retitle his *Otello as Iago,* because of the high regard he and others had for Rossini's version of *Otello.*) Compromises such as this were common for composers then. Rossini spun out his operas in much the same way a writer today whips out a script for a TV series—fast, furiously and with whatever he could put to good use. He cheerfully borrowed from himself to fill in here and there, and he left the writing of the recitatives to someone else. Despite all the privation that surrounded him, Rossini seems to have been in good spirits when he composed the opera. He was surrounded by a fine cast that pulled together in a desperate situation, and it is difficult to listen to the music and not imagine Rossini laughing as he wrote. The most convincing accounts suggest that a total of 24 days elapsed between the conception of *The Barber of Seville* and its premiere. At best, Rossini had a little more than two weeks to actually compose the music, which amounted to 600 pages of manuscript. Scholars have tracked down the many places in the score for *The Barber of Seville* where he stole from his own earlier works, usually just a melody or a phrase. Some have found echoes of Haydn and Spontini in the score, and even a Russian folk song.

The most famous contingency in the score for *The Barber of Seville,* though, is its most famous feature—the overture. Rossini apparently wrote an original overture for the opera but it was lost. In its place, he used an overture that had already served him not once but *twice* in earlier operas, both of them dramas—*Aureliano in Pamira* and *Elisabetta, Regina d'Inghilterra,* for which he added some military-sounding embellishments. He removed those for *The Barber of Seville,* where the overture came to rest finally and fortuitously. It is an ironic twist, for the bustling overture seems the perfect embodiment of the intrigue, slapstick and buoyant good will of *The Barber of Seville,* crowned by one of Rossini's thrilling, trademark crescendos. After all this frantic preparation, the opening night was a disaster. Murphy's Law hit overdrive. Topping off a performance filled with more than its share gaffes and miscues, an itinerant cat padded onto the stage

DAME NELLIE MELBA (1861-1931) AS ROSINA.

during the finale, mingling with the frazzled cast and leaving the indifferent audience hysterical with laughter and meowing at the cat as the singers bravely tried to do their job. Geltrude Righetti-Georgi, a childhood friend of Rossini's

who came out of retirement to create the role of Rosina, reported that the composer was devastated, and who could blame him? Curiously, as was the case with the Beaumarchais play (which also opened to derision), the public response completely reversed itself in a matter of days. *The Barber of Seville* delighted its second audience, and its appeal has grown ever since.

Such a story tells us a lot about the composer and the musical world he inhabited. In our time, Rossini is a much misunderstood composer because he does not conform to our idea of an artist. Though he lived to the age of 75, he essentially retired when he was 37, after composing nearly 40 operas. He was rich, happy and universally beloved, and he simply decided to enjoy the rest of his life in luxurious comfort, first in Bologna, then in Paris where he became the merry *eminence grise* of musical life. The photos we have of Rossini come from this period, and you can see in his face just how content he was—a slight smile, a light in his eyes, an air of well-being, crowning a stout figure that bespeaks the good life. (There is an obvious reason why the gourmet dish known as tournedos Rossini came into being.) He was, first and foremost, a man of the theater, with a shrewd sense of how to please an audience. Perhaps, in 1829, Rossini sensed the coming revolution in opera, signaled by the innovations of Weber and Meyerbeer, later fully realized by the genius of Verdi and Wagner. His last opera, *William Tell,* is one of his masterpieces, a noble and stupendous work that definitely points to the future—Wagnerian in its scope and dimensions, Verdian in its incisive characterization and narrative.

But Rossini was an entertainer, not a philosopher, and he was just the kind of figure the emerging Romantic era would might a bit foolish and passé. He wrote operas to make money, as much money as he could possibly negotiate, and he needed money to support himself in the style he desired. His operas have a patented sound; as we have seen, they frequently even share bits of the same music. There are French and Italian versions of several of his operas, because he was happy to adapt them variously to meet the demands of the moment. (Verdi would have to do the same thing, though a good deal less cheerfully.) Rossini believed himself to be an artist but also a showman, and he barely dreamed of the kind of artistic autonomy Verdi and Wagner would one day expect as their due. It simply did not exist in his world, as it did not exist in Mozart's. Would he have liked it? Certainly. But he seemed to know that his time had passed, and he graciously passed into legend, a status he enjoyed immensely.

Aside from the brilliance of the work itself, the reason for the consistent popularity of *The Barber of Seville* has been its popularity with singers. The original cast boasted a bona fide legend—the Spanish tenor Manuel Garcia, who created the role of Count Almaviva and made a specialty of it. Garcia later became the most famous voice teacher of his day and was the first to develop and teach a technique for vocal development. He was also the father of two legendary singers, Maria Malibran and Pauline Viardot-Garcia. One of the most beautiful and entrancing divas

PAULINE VIARDOT-GARCIA, 1863

of what we now call the bel canto era, Malibran once sang Rosina to her father's Almaviva, but she died tragically young. Viardot-Garcia was a comparatively homely woman, but she became an equally famous singer in Paris in the mid-19th century. She was also brilliant, with a compelling personality, and she was almost as potent a figure in Parisian musical society as Rossini himself. He invited her to sing the mezzo-soprano solos in the first, private performance of portions of his setting of the *Stabat Mater.*

Vocal styles changed a great deal after Rossini's retirement. He understood the voice very well, even if his writing tested the limits of what singers could do. But the elegant, graceful style of singing he and his contemoparies Bellini and Donizetti knew and catered to—bel canto, it was later dubbed—was undergoing a transformation. Singing had to become more forceful, more pungent and simply louder, to accommodate the demands of Romantic opera. As a composer, Rossini had an unpleasant taste of this after the premiere of *William Tell.* Tenors had just begun then to develop the technique of singing their high notes with chest resonance, instead of projecting them in a lighter "head" voice that almost sounds like a falsetto. Rossini was skeptical. When he heard the tenor Gilbert Duprez sing the tenor aria from *William Tell* with trumpeted high Cs sung from the chest, he was aghast, reportedly describing the sound as that of "a capon having its head cut off." Years later, the young soprano Adelina Patti—the greatest diva of the latter half of the 19th century—came to one of Rossini's famous musicales in Paris and sang Rosina's "Una voce poco fa" from *The Barber of Seville,* with her own elaborate embellishments. Rossini was appalled, and he devastated Patti by sarcastically wondering aloud who had written the piece she had just sung. The composer Camille Saint-Saëns wrote that, days later, Rossini was still fuming about the incident. He told Saint-Saëns that, while some decoration of the vocal line was to be expected, Patti had made the aria unrecognizable. In the same conversation, he complained about the growing attraction sopranos had for the role of Rosina, which he had intended for a mezzo-soprano—an attraction that persists to this day.

The legacy of all this makes *The Barber of Seville* an irresistible but in some ways elusive opera in the modern world, despite the attraction of the music. The recording you will hear was the first truly complete recording of the score. The singing is definitely on the modern scale: Rossini might be non-plussed by the booming splendor of Sherrill Milnes' Figaro and the crisp, ringing sound of tenor Nicolai Gedda's Almaviva. The recording also departs from strict historical accuracy, as the composer might have complained, by featuring a lyric soprano as Rosina. But Beverly Sills (who was the primary reason for this recording) was following a long tradition of sopranos singing the role. From Patti forward, it has been as much a staple for such sopranos as Luisa Tetrazzini, Amelita Galli-Curci, Toti dal Monte, Lina Pagliughi, Lily Pons, Roberta Peters, Kathleen Battle and Ruth Ann Swenson. At the same time, mezzo-sopranos such as Conchita Supervia, Giulietta Simionato, Teresa Berganza, Marilyn Horne, Frederica von Stade, Suzanne Mentzer, Cecilia Bartoli, Jennifer Larmore and Vesselina Kasarova have had brilliant successes in the role, as well.

In the end, these are just details in the service of genius. Rossini's fame and popularity might have been eclipsed by Verdi, Wagner, Puccini and others. We might view his operas with polite fascination, as splendid objects from another time and place, fabulous and transcendently beautiful antiques. But *The Barber of Seville* endures, evergreen and perfect, a comedy that merrily defies the passage of time. After almost 200 years of relentless performances, if you listen carefully through the music, you might still hear Rossini laughing.

The Story of The Barber of Seville

ACT I

Scene 1

It is early morning in the Spanish city of Seville, and the first rays of sunlight spread across a sleepy square to the outside walls of the home of Don Bartolo. The servant Fiorello beckons a group of musicians-for-hire into the square, where they quietly prepare to play. With them is Count Almaviva, and they accompany him in a morning serenade beneath the window of Rosina, the lovely young ward of Don Bartolo. In his song, the Count beckons Rosina to end his torment and surrender to his love. But Rosina does not seem to have heard the him. He abandons his serenade, telling Fiorello to pay the musicians and send them away. The musicians are a little too noisy in expressing their gratitude, and it takes both the Count and Fiorello to get rid of them without disturbing the neighbors. The Count has not given up hope that Rosina will appear. He lingers in the square until he hears a raucous voice in the distance, which causes him to run for cover. The singer is Figaro, the indefatigable barber (and factotum, or know-it-all) of Seville going about his business. Figaro savors his amazing ability to be all things to all people, all of the time. The Count emerges from his hiding place when he realizes it is his subject Figaro, who is astonished to see his master under such circumstances. The nobleman swears Figaro to secrecy and tells the servant he is infatuated with the beautiful Rosina, whom he has been following since he first saw her in Madrid. Always in the know, Figaro is able to fill in the details for the Count...after all, Figaro is a frequent visitor to Don Bartolo's home. Their chat is interrupted when Rosina emerges on the balcony. She carries with her a letter. Before she and the Count can find each other, Bartolo joins her to greet the morning; seeing the letter, he demands to know what it says. Just the words of an aria from a romantic opera called *The Futile Precaution,* she slyly tells Bartolo, as she lets the letter slip from her fingers to the street below. Bartolo is appalled by her indiscreet taste in opera and heads for the street to find the page, though the Count beats him to it. Suspecting a ruse, Bartolo hustles Rosina back into the house. When Figaro reads the letter to the Count, it reveals Rosina's interest. But, it asks, could she know who he is and what he intends? The Count's joy is short-lived, for Bartolo emerges from his home, bursting with the news that he is to marry Rosina later that day. As he leaves to finalize the plans, Figaro and the Count decide another serenade is in order. He informs her in his song that he is the poor but ardent Lindoro. She is charmed and responds to him, singing from behind the shutters of her rooms, though she suddenly breaks off. The Count is elated. Can Figaro help him get into the house? The servant's ears immediately perk up when he learns there will be a handsome reward for him. Figaro tells the Count that a regiment is expected in town, led by a colonel he knows, and that he can arrange for Bartolo to be required to billet the troops, which could include the

THE ROYAL OPERA HOUSE IN LONDON, COVENT GARDEN.

disguised Count. Figaro suggests his lord act like a drunkard, for good measure, since Bartolo is less inclined to suspect a man in such a condition. They agree to meet at Figaro's shop to seal the deal—the Count a lover fulfilled, Figaro a little richer in the bargain.

Scene 2

In the courtyard of Bartolo's house, Rosina is holding yet another response to Lindoro. She is determined to be with him, in spite of Bartolo's ridiculous expectations, and she begins plotting how to make it happen. With the exquisite timing that is his alone, Figaro turns up just as she is pondering her problem. But before they can discuss a solution, Bartolo enters, fuming at Figaro that the barber/surgeon's cures and remedies have only succeeded in making the entire household sick: the servants Berta and Ambrogio can't stop yawning and sneezing. Rosina has slipped away in the midst of this encounter, but her music teacher Don Basilio suddenly arrives. He can't wait to tell Bartolo that his rival for Rosina's hand—Count Almaviva—has been spotted in Seville. Basilio calms Bartolo with the assurance that he can handle the situation, through the devilish workings of calumny. Bartolo decides to rush the marriage contract; Basilio is happy to oblige, if the price is right. Figaro has overheard all of this and tells Rosina. She wants to know who it was she saw Figaro with earlier. His poor cousin, he tells her, who is dying of love for none other than her. He tells her that Lindoro only needs a line or two from her to convince him of her love. She sends Figaro off with the letter written earlier. Bartolo enters, full of suspicions about Figaro, the ink stains of Rosina's fingers, a missing sheet of paper...Rosina tries to explain, but Bartolo is not fooled. He doubles the guard on her door and both leave in a fury. Berta answers a knock at the door. The Count enters, in disguise and playing the drunkard. He presents Bartolo with his billet, scanning the room for a sign of Rosina. An angry Bartolo looks for the papers that exempt him from billeting troops, while Rosina appears and the drunken soldier reveals himself to her as Lindoro. A comedy of errors ensues: Bartolo finds the exemption, the Count knocks it out of his hand while he passes a note to Rosina, which she exchanges for a laundry list before Bartolo can demand to see it. She begins to cry at Bartolo's anger, the Count berates Bartolo, and Berta enters with Basilio to add to the confusion. The sudden but timely arrival of Figaro calms the scene momentarily, until the real billeted soldiers arrive, joined by curious neighbors drawn by the disturbance. The officer leading the regiment is about to arrest the Count as an imposter, until the Count shows him a document that draws from the officer a salute. Everyone begins to wonder aloud about the insane turn of events, which is so bizarre that it has them all spellbound and completely frazzled.

Act II

That masquerading "soldier" has vanished, of course, but Bartolo is sure he was an agent of Count Almaviva. Bartolo's inquiries have yielded nothing. He is in the music room of his house, planning his next step, when a knock at the door announces one Don Alonso, an unexpected guest who is, in fact, the Count in yet another disguise. Bartolo does not recognize him but is still suspicious. Alonso tells Bartolo that he is a student of Basilio's, whom he says is ill; Alonso has come to give Rosina her voice lesson. What's more, he presents to Bartolo Rosina's letter to the Count, which he says he can use to make Rosina think the Count is faithless. Such a scheme proves to Bartolo that Alonso is indeed Basilio's student, and he brings Rosina in for her lesson. She recognizes her Lindoro immediately, though she reveals this to him secretly, by choosing the aria from *The Futile Precaution* for her voice lesson. Alonso praises Rosina's voice, but Bartolo is appalled by the brazenness of the aria. He suggests something more discreet, which he demonstrates, as Figaro enters and mimics him behind his back. Bartolo wheels on Figaro, wanting to know why he has arrived. To give Bartolo a shave, of course, Figaro tells him. Bartolo reluctantly goes to find towels, when Figaro asks Rosina for the key to the outside window. Suspicious of Figaro, Bartolo returns and sends the barber himself to get the towels. Figaro stages a diversion, sending Bartolo running out of the room, and that allows him to return with the correct key for the Count. Then Basilio turns up, and the whole ruse threatens to collapse until the Count bribes the music teacher, who leaves happy with his bag of gold coins. Figaro resumes shaving Bartolo, and the Count tells Rosina he will meet her that night. But Bartolo overhears the plan and chases them all away in a rage. The tired old servant Berta complains about the noise but realizes that love is behind it all and that even she is susceptible to its allure. Bartolo re-enters with Basilio, who is convinced Alonso was actually the Count. When he learns Figaro is searching for a notary for the marriage of his "niece," Bartolo tries to head him off by sending Basilio to obtain the notary instead. But he is not finished: Bartolo still has Rosina's letter, which Alonso gave him, and he uses it to convince Rosina that the Count/Lindoro is faithless. She is devastated, and she explains the whole plot to the grimly satisfied Bartolo. A storm shatters the evening calm but it fades in time for Figaro and the Count to slip over the wall for their rescue of Rosina. She is furious with her beloved, whom she now believes has deceived her. Lindoro calms her by explaining that he is Count Almaviva. Figaro tries to speed the reconciled lovers over the wall, only to discover their ladder has been removed. They hide. Basilio arrives with the notary, but the Count intervenes. He makes Basilio an offer he cannot refuse to witness the signing of the contract, only by Rosina and the Count. Bartolo has soldiers with him when he bursts in to stop the marriage, but he is outclassed, outstripped and outranked by the Count. The old man finally gives up but feels a bit better when the Count offers him a handsome dowry for Rosina's hand. The Count, Rosina and the newly enriched Figaro exult in their triumph, and everyone joins them in best wishes for the happily-ever-after future of the Count and his new Countess.

The Barber of Seville

GIOACCHINO ROSSINI 1792-1868

Rosina..Beverly Sills
Il Conte d'Almaviva...Nicolai Gedda
Figaro..Sherrill Milnes
Bartolo..Renato Capecchi
Basilio...Ruggero Raimondi
Berta..Fedora Barbieri
Fiorello..Joseph Galiano
Ambrogio/Uffizialer..Michael Rippon

Conducted by James Levine
London Symphony Orchestra
John Alldis Choir
Chorus Master: John Alldis

The Performers

BEVERLY SILLS (Rosina) has been perhaps one of the most popular and influential American musicians of the 20th century. Born in Brooklyn as Belle Miriam Silverman, she was the daughter of immigrants, an insurance salesman and a woman with musical interests who put her in show business as a baby. At the age of 3, she won a radio

BEVERLY SILLS AND HER DAUGHTER, WHO IS DEAF.

contest in Brooklyn as "the most beautiful baby of 1932." Nicknamed "Bubbles," she grew up singing in commercials and performing on the radio. Her vocal studies began when she was 7, as a student of Estelle Liebling, and she made her operatic debut at the Philadelphia Civic Opera in 1947 as Frasquita in a production of *Carmen*. Sills built her career without going to

Europe—almost unheard of for a serious American singer in the 1950s—singing with a number of important American opera companies, including the San Francisco Opera in 1953 and, two years later, the New York City Opera. She would remain on the New York City Opera roster for the next 25 years, during which the company emerged from the shadow of the more glamorous Metropolitan Opera and established its own artistic identity. With conductor Julius Rudel, Sills was a key element in that transformation, a singing actress of formidable skill and wide-ranging virtuosity who led the company's superb and loyal ensemble of American singers. Her repertoire was all-embracing, a testament to her intelligence, musicianship and passion. She memorably created the title role in Douglas Moore's *The Ballad of Baby Doe* and even sang in American performances of Luigi Nono's post-serialist opera *Intolleranza*. But her true metier was in 19th-century opera, primarily Italian *bel canto* and French roles. Her voice was essentially a lyric soprano, with great flexibility and range, though she enjoyed some of her great successes in more dramatic roles. In 1966 at City Opera, she had a career breakthrough as Cleopatra in Handel's *Julius Caesar,* and she became increasingly more identified with the revival of interest in *bel canto* opera. Along with Dame Joan Sutherland and Montserrat Caballé, she championed the operas of Bellini, Donizetti and Rossini, putting her own personal stamp on the leading roles in *Lucia di Lammermoor, Norma, Don Pasquale, La Fille du Regiment, L'Assedio di Corinto* and Donizetti's "Tudor queen trilogy"—*Anna Bolena, Maria Stuarda* and *Roberto Devereux.* She also triumphed in the title role of Massenet's *Manon,* as the three heroines of Offenbach's *Les contes d'Hoffmann* and as Violetta in *La Traviata.* Sills' career went international in the late 1960s with successful debuts at Teatro Colón in Buenos Aires, Deutsche Oper in Berlin and La Scala in Milan. Her Metropolitan Opera debut came, at the height of her fame, in 1975 as Pamira in

L'Assedio di Corinto. Throughout the 1970s, she was known as America's "queen of opera," appearing frequently on TV and enjoying a belated international recording career. Following her retirement, Sills served with distinction as general director of NewYork City Opera, from which she in 1988, and she later served as chair of LincolnCenter for the Performing Arts.

Nicolai Gedda (Almaviva/Lindoro) has become the model of the modern tenor, equally at home on the opera, recital and concert stages, a sophisticated singer equipped with a firm but flexible technique that has allowed him to encompass a repertoire almost unprecedented in its breadth. He was born in Stockholm in 1925 to a Swedish mother and a Russian father (who was a bass in the Don Cossack Choir) and spent part of his childhood in Leipzig. His gift for languages was a key factor in his early success, making his professional debut in Stockholm in 1952 in the title role of Adam's *Le Postillon de Longjumeau.* Walter Legge of EMI Records happened to hear Gedda during a Stockholm visit that year and, noting his linguistic skill as well as his brilliant lyric tenor voice, immediately signed him for an upcoming recording of *Boris Godunov.* Major European debuts followed quickly, as Gedda established himself with a succession of important recordings for EMI. In addition to opera, he was recognized as a distin-

SWEDISH TENOR NICOLAI GEDDA

guished lieder singer and oratorio soloist. After his Metropolitan Opera debut in 1957, he created the title role in the company's world premiere of Samuel Barber's *Vanessa* the following year. For the next 30 years, Gedda sang operatic roles as diverse as the boyish Nemorino in *L'Elisir d'amore* and the heroic title part in Wagner's *Lohengrin*. Later in his career, he took on Russian roles and explored unusual areas of the song repertoire, with occasional forays into novelty like composer-conductor Leonard Bernstein's definitive recording of his musical *Candide*.

SHERRILL MILNES (Figaro) has been an important link in the 20th-century tradition that one pundit has called "the prairie baritone"—an American baritone with a big, powerful, richly dark sound, with ringing high notes and a self-confidence that almost has a cowboy's swagger. When he came on the scene in mid-1960s, Milnes joined a line of baritones that included Lawrence Tibbett, John Charles Thomas, Leonard Warren and Robert Merrill, and also inspired such pop singers as John Raitt, Howard Keel and Gordon MacRae. Milnes was born in Downers Grove, Ill., and decided to become a singer after beginning a medical degree. He studied at Drake University and Northwestern University, and sang in choral performances in the Chicago area. After apprenticing at the Santa Fe Opera, Milnes joined teacher/director Boris Goldovsky's opera ensemble in 1960 and, the following year, met the retired diva Rosa Ponselle. Ponselle coached him in several roles and, at Baltimore Civic Opera, sponsored his debut as Carlo Gérard in *Andrea Chénier*. He made his European debut in 1964 as Figaro in *The Barber of Seville* at Milan's Teatro Nuovo, but returned to the U.S. almost immediately to make his New York City Opera debut as Valentin in *Faust*. His Metropolitan Opera debut, again as Valentin, came on December 22, 1965, beginning a relationship that would stretch over three decades. As Robert

Merrill's stage career at the Met came to an end, Milnes assumed many of his signature roles, with particular acclaim in such Verdi operas as *Rigoletto, La Traviata, Un Ballo in Maschera, Aida, Don Carlo, Il Trovatore, I Vespri Siciliani, Simon Boccanegra* and *Otello* as well as Valentin, Rossini's Figaro, as Carlo Gérard and in baritone roles in *La Gioconda, Pagliacci, La Fanciulla del West* and *Thaïs.* During the 1970s, Milnes was a mainstay at the Met, as well as the most celebrated American and international companies, and he recorded extensively, often with tenor Plácido Domingo. In the 1990s, Milnes began concentrating on leading character roles such as Amonasro in *Aida* and Scarpia in *Tosca,* and even the title role in Verdi's *Falstaff.*

RENATO CAPECCHI (Don Bartolo) enjoyed an uncommonly long career as baritone, first in leading lyric and Verdi roles, then as a character singer. Born in Cairo to Italian parents, he studied voice in Milan and made his stage debut in 1948 at Reggio Emilia, as Amonasro in Aida. Capecchi joined the La Scala company in 1950 and bowed the following year at the Metropolitan Opera as Giorgio Germont in La Traviata. He later made a notable appearance in the title role of *Don Giovanni* at the Aix-en-Provence festival, but enjoyed an even more telling success in 1955 as Don Bartolo in *The Barber of Seville* at the Arena di Verona. This signaled the beginning of his career as an impeccable buffa singer, his fine voice allied with a wonderful comic sense and solid stage skills. Capecchi was also memorable as Fra Melitone in *La Forza del Destino,* the title roles in *Falstaff* (in which he also sang the role of Ford) and *Gianni Schicchi, Don Pasquale* and even *The Barber of Seville,* in which he was a celebrated Figaro. He also sang the role of Figaro in Mozart's *The Marriage of Figaro,* as well as both Sgt. Belcore and Dr. Dulcamara in *L'Elisir d'amore.*

RUGGERO RAIMONDI (Don Basilio) has been one of the finest singing actors of his generation, enjoying a career of distinction, particularly in Mozart and Verdi, virtually since he began singing professionally. Born in Bologna in 1941 and educated at Rome's Accademia di Santa Cecilia, the Italian bass made his debut in 1964 at the Spoleto Festival as Colline in Puccini's *La Bohème*. He joined the roster at Milan's La Scala three years later, with his Metropolitan Opera debut following in the fall of 1970, as Silva in *Ernani*. Raimondi has won particular acclaim for his portrayals of King Philip II in *Don Carlo,* Figaro in *The Marriage of Figaro* and the title roles in *Don Giovanni* and *Boris Godunov.* The suave, theatrical intensity of his performances has been a career trademark, to such a degree that conductor Herbert von Karajan convinced to undertake the nominally baritone role of Scarpia—in a tour de force portrayal of uncommonly sinister elegance—for the maestro's final recording of *Tosca.* Raimondi has also triumphed in two internationally acclaimed film versions of operas, as Escamillo in Francesco Rosi's *Carmen* (1984) and in the title role of Joseph Losey's *Don Giovanni* (1979). His film performances were so successful that he went on to act in non-musical Italian films. But opera, both on the stage and in recordings, has been his true metier, in a career remarkable for its breadth and consistency, paralleling that of his frequent colleague, tenor Plácido Domingo.

FEDORA BARBIERI (Berta) was in the twilight of her career when she made this recording, taking a role usually sung by a comprimario because of the inclusion of the maid's rarely performed aria. Barbieri was one of the leading Italian mezzo-sopranos of the 1940s and 1950s—following in the distinctive tradition of such great mezzo divas as Lina Bruna Rasa and Ebe Stignani—best known to most listeners for memorably partnering Maria Callas in classic recordings of *Aida* (as Amneris) and *Il Trovatore* (as Azucena). A native of Trieste, she made her professional debut in Florence in 1940, at the age of 20, singing throughout Europe during early years of World War II. She briefly retired after marrying in 1943, but returned to the stage in Florence in 1945 with a portrayal of Azucena that signaled the emergence of a major talent. Barbieri's international career blossomed in the late 1940s to include regular visits to the major companies in Paris, Vienna, London, Buenos Aires, New York , San Francisco and Chicago, and she enjoyed a long, distinguished affiliation with La Scala in Milan. She sang most of the leading mezzo-soprano and contralto roles in Italian opera and was also acclaimed for her performance in the title role of *Carmen.*

JAMES LEVINE has been a dominant figure in the world of opera in the last quarter of the 20th century, both as a versatile conductor and as the vigorous artistic leader of the Metropolitan Opera at a decisive stage in its history. He has become the model of the modern maestro, formidably and prodigiously talented, indefatigable, ambitious and at home at the helm of any of the world's best orchestras and opera companies. Born in Cincinnati in 1943 to a pop musician and an actress, Levine was a child prodigy who studied piano with Rudolf Serkin and Rosina Lhevinne before entering the Juilliard School of Music in 1961. His first coaching as a conductor came at Juilliard from Jean Morel, and he also studied with Wolfgang Vacano at the Aspen Festival. After an early apprenticeship in Baltimore, Levine spent five years as an assistant conductor to George Szell at the Cleveland Orchestra. In 1970, his career expanded through conducting debuts with the Philadelphia Orchestra, Welsh National Opera and San Francisco Opera. In June of 1971, at the age of 27, he conducted a Metropolitan Opera performance for the first time, an outdoor post-season *Tosca*. Further appearances during the following subscription season led to his appointment as the company's first principal conductor. As the management structure of the Met began to change, Levine began to assume more responsibility, taking over as music director in 1975, after Rafael Kubelik's resignation. His influence there expanded even more over the next decade, culminating in his appointment as the company's artistic director in 1986. Levine's role at the Met has been unprecedented in its century-plus history. He has conducted a lion's share of the company's new productions and major revivals while also transforming its orchestra and chorus, now arguably the world's finest. With that success came criticism, but Levine endured and earned much of the credit for his tireless efforts to modernize and popularize the Met and its mission. In his summers off from the Met, he has also led memorable performances at the Salzburg and Bayreuth Festivals. At the same time, Levine has maintained a distinguished career conducting and recording symphonic music with the world's leading orchestras since the 1970s. As a pianist, he also continues to perform chamber music and accompany vocal and instrumental soloists. Under his direction, the Met's orchestra has become an outstanding symphonic ensemble, on the model of the Vienna Philharmonic, and late in 1997 he was named musical director of the Munich Philharmonic. In opera, Levine has been particularly acclaimed for his brilliant, propulsive interpretations of Verdi and Wagner, as well as such 20th-century masterpieces as Berg's *Wozzeck* and *Lulu*.

The Libretto

Act 1

Scene 1

A square in Seville

Overture Ta-da! Thus begins the most famous of all operatic overtures. Those famous chords are followed by a rising "question-and-answer" sequence that is repeated in the strings and winds, from which the oboe saves a moment of tension by leading the way into a new section where the violins sing a graceful new melody over pizzicato (plucked) low strings (00:53). The dialogue of the opening returns (01:23), with a new element of tension that is confirmed suddenly by forceful chords that echo the overture's opening notes. The atmosphere turns breathlessly urgent (02:01) with a new, melodramatic tune in the minor that seems to sputter angrily, pause to reinforce itself (in the woodwinds) and press on again, exploding finally in a fury (02:31) that spreads throughout the entire orchestra with a fierceness that echoes Beethoven. This "storm" evaporates in the trilling of the violins, carrying the music into the major (03:28) and a suddenly upbeat atmosphere. Over the pulsing of the strings, the oboe pipes a jaunty tune that draws comments from the other winds and the strings. An air of expectation rises from this new mood, with the strings and woodwinds beginning to chatter (04:15) with ever-increasing excitement that finally seems to spend itself. And we are back (04:57) in a sleek restatement of the little musical conflict that was just played. The jaunty little tune returns, with greater brilliance, and it is followed by the chattering of the strings and woodwinds. This time, though, the atmosphere is more exultant Even the orchestra's crescendo is grander, breaking out at last with a fresh, festive, dance-like melody (06:35) that possesses the entire orchestra. The frenzy grows and grows, mischievously scaling back (07:01) for a brief second, to allow yet another joyous crescendo sweep the overture to its triumphant conclusion.

(To the left is the house with balcony of Don Bartolo. The time is dawn. Fiorello, with a lantern in his hand, introduces various musicians; then Count Almaviva, wrapped up in a mantle.)

FIORELLO
Piano, pianissimo, senza parlar,
tutti con me venite qua.

SUONATORI
Piano, pianissimo, eccoci qua.

FIORELLO
Tutto è silenzio, nessun qui sta
che i nostri canti possa turbar.

FIORELLO
Piano, pianissimo, without a word
all gather around me here.

MUSICIANS
Piano, pianissimo, here we are.

FIORELLO
All is silence, no one is near
our songs to disturb.

(Count Almaviva, wrapped in a cloak, enters.)

CONTE
Fiorello...Olà!

FIORELLO
Signor, son qua.

CONTE
Ebben!...gli amici?

FIORELLO
Son pronti già.

COUNT
Fiorello...ho!

FIORELLO
Sir, I am here.

COUNT
Well!...and our friends?

FIORELLO
They are all ready.

(He crosses to the musicians.)

CONTE
Bravi, bravissimi, fate silenzio;
piano, pianissimo, senza parlar.

SUONATORI
Piano, pianissimo, senza parlar.

COUNT
Bravi, bravissimi, softly, softly;
piano, pianissimo, utter no word.

MUSICIANS
Piano, pianissimo, without a word.

FIORELLO
Senza parlar, venite qua.

CONTE
Piano, senza parlar.

FIORELLO
Without a word, without a word.

COUNT
Piano, utter no word.

(The musicians tune their instruments, and the Count sings, accompanied by them.)

disc no. 1/track 3 *Ecco ridente il cielo!* The overture's opening chords introduce the accompaniment of the musicians Fiorello has assembled, with woodwinds singing the melody of the Count's serenade over the strumming of the guitar. The Count begins to sing the melody (01:05), beckoning Rosina to come to him. The gentle tune becomes more and more ardent until he thinks he sees her (02:47). The Count erupts into rollicking little expressions of pleasure (in elaborate and decorative phrases called fioritura), echoed in the orchestra. He pauses to wonder at the miracle of love (03:33), before getting carried away once again. He is a man possessed with love, his giddy delight all but bubbling out of him, with his joy carrying him up to an ecstatic high C (04:38).

Ecco ridente in cielo
spunta la bella aurora,
e tu non sorgi ancora
e puoi dormir così?
Sorgi, mia dolce speme,
vieni bell'idol mio,
rendi men crudo, oh Dio,
lo stral che mi ferì.
Oh sorte! già veggo
quel caro sembiante,
quest'anima amante
ottenne pietà!
Oh, istante d'amore!
Felice momento!
Oh, dolce contento
che egual non ha!
Ehi, Fiorello?

Lo, in the smiling sky,
the lovely dawn is breaking,
and you are not awake,
and you are still asleep?
Arise, my sweetest love,
oh, come, my treasured one,
soften the pain, O God,
of the dart which pierces me.
Oh, joy! Do I now see
that dearest vision,
has she taken pity
on this soul in love?
Oh, moment of love!
Oh, moment divine!
Oh, sweet content
which is unequalled!
Ho, Fiorello!

FIORELLO
Mio signore...

CONTE
Di', la vedi?

FIORELLO
Signor no.

CONTE
Ah, ch'è vana ogni speranza!

FIORELLO
Signor Conte, il giorno avanza.

CONTE
Ah, che penso! Che farò?
Tutto è vano. Buona gente!

SUONATORI (*sottovoce*)
Mio signor...

FIORELLO
M'lord...

COUNT
Say, have you seen her?

FIORELLO
No, sir.

COUNT
Ah, how vain is every hope!

FIORELLO
Behold, sir, the dawn advances.

COUNT
Ah, what am I to think! what shall I do?
All is vain. Well, my friends!

MUSICIANS (*softly*)
M'lord...

(The Count is in despair; he dismisses the musicians.)

CONTE
Avanti, avanti.

COUNT
Retire, retire.

(He gives a purse to Fiorello, who distributes money to all.)

Più di suoni, più di canti
io bisogno ormai non ho.

I have no longer need
of your songs or your music.

FIORELLO
Buona notte a tutti quanti.
Più di voi che far non so.

FIORELLO
Good night all.
I have nothing further for you to do.

(The musicians surround the Count, thanking him and kissing his hand. Annoyed by the noise they make, he tries to drive them away. Fiorello does the same.)

SUONATORI

Mille grazie, mio signore,
del favore, dell'onore.
Ah! di tanta cortesia
obbligati in verità!
Oh, che incontro fortunato!
È un signore di qualità.

CONTE

Basta, basta, non parlate,
ma non serve, non gridate,
maledetti, andate via!
Ah, canaglia, via di qua!
Tutto quanto il vicinato
questo chiasso sveglierà.

FIORELLO

Zitti, zitti, che rumore!
Maledetti, via di qua!
Ve' che chiasso indiavolato,
ah, che rabbia che mi fa!
Maledetti, andate via,
ah, canaglia, via di qua!

MUSICIANS

Many thanks, sir, for this favour;
better master, nor a braver,
ever did we sing a stave for.
Pray, good sir, command our throats!
We will sing and pray for
one who gives us gold for notes!

COUNT

Silence! Silence! Cease your bawling,
nor, like cats with caterwauling
wake the neighbours - stop your squalling.
Rascals, get away from here!
If this noise you still keep making,
all the neighbours you'll be waking.

FIORELLO

Silence! Silence! What an uproar!
Cursed ones, away from here!
What a devilish commotion,
I am furious, do you hear!
Cursed ones, get out, get out,
scoundrels all, away from here!

(Fiorello manages to push the musicians slowly out of the piazza.)

CONTE

Gente indiscreta!

FIORELLO

Ah, quasi con quel chiasso importuno
tutto quanto il quartiere
han risvegliato.
Alfin sono partiti.

CONTE *(guardando verso il balcone)*

E non si vede! È inutile sperar.

COUNT

Indiscreet rabble!

FIORELLO

They had nearly,
with their importunate clamour,
awakened the whole neighbourhood.
At last they're gone!

COUNT *(looking up at the balcony)*

I can't see her. It's useless to hope.

(Eppur qui voglio aspettar di vederla.
Ogni mattina ella su quel balcone
a prender fresco viene in sull'aurora.
Proviamo.)
Olà, tu ancora ritirati, Fiorel.

FIORELLO
Vado. Là in fondo attenderò i suoi ordini.

(He withdraws.)

CONTE
Con lei se parlar mi riesce,
non voglio testimoni.
Che a quest'ora io tutti i giorni
qui vengo per lei dev'essersi avveduta.
Oh, vedi, amore a un uomo del
mio rango comme l'ha fatta bella!
Eppure, eppure! oh! dev'esser mia sposa.

FIGARO *(dietro le quinte)*
La la la la la la la la la.

CONTE
Chi è mai quest'importuno?
Lasciamolo passar;
sotto quegli archi non veduto
vedrò quanto bisogna.
Già l'alba appare e amor non si vergogna.

(Yet I will wait here to glimpse her.
Every morning at dawn she comes out
on that balcony to take the air.
Let's try.)
Ho, there, Fiorello, you can go.

FIORELLO
I'm off. I'll await your orders over there.

COUNT
If I manage to talk to her
I don't want witnesses.
She must have noticed that I come
here every day at this time to see her.
Oh, just see what love has done
to a man of my rank!
Yet, yet...oh, she must be my bride...

FIGARO *(offstage)*
La la la la la la la la.

COUNT
Who is this coming now?
I'll let him go by;
unseen, under this archway,
I can see what I want.
Dawn is already here but love is not shy.

(He hides. Figaro enters with a guitar around his neck.)

disc no. 1/track 7 *La ran la le ra...Largo al factotum* A vigorous figure in the orchestra announces Figaro's arrival, with the bubbling of the woodwinds serving as his fanfare. Happily singing a stream of nonsense, he is on his way to work. Make way for factotum, he sings happily (00:35), for he is Figaro, a happy man who knows how to ply his trade...and, of course, enjoy the occasional pleasure on the side (01: 57). Proudly he enumerates the varied talents for which everyone in Seville—man, woman and child—relies on him. He describes the chaos he encounters on a daily basis, mimicking the cries for assistance he hears all the time. Then, with a hero's bravura (03:57), he recounts how smoothly, surely and quickly he dispatches his many tasks.

FIGARO	**FIGARO**
La ran la le ra, la ran la la.	La ran la le ra, la ran la la.
Largo al factotum della città!	Make way for the factotum of the city.
La ran la la, ecc.	La ran la la, etc.
Presto a bottega	Rushing to his shop
che l'alba è già.	for dawn is here.
La ran la la, ecc.	La ran la la, etc.
Ah, che bel vivere,	What a merry life,
che bel piacere,	what gay pleasures
per un barbiere	for a barber
di qualità.	of quality.
Ah, bravo Figaro,	Ah, bravo Figaro,
bravo, bravissimo, bravo!	bravo, bravissimo, bravo!
La ran la la, ecc.	La ran la la, etc.
Fortunatissimo	Most fortunate of men,
per verità. Bravo!	indeed you are!
La ran la la, ecc.	La ran la la, etc.
Pronto a far tutto	Ready for everything
la notte, il giorno,	by night or by day,
sempre d'intorno	always in bustle,
in giro sta.	in constant motion.
Miglior cuccagna	A better lot
per un barbiere,	for a barber,
vita più nobile,	a nobler life
no, non si dà.	does not exist.
La la ran la la ran la, ecc.	La la ran la la ran la, etc.
Rasori e pettini,	Razors and combs,
lancette e forbici,	lancets and scissors,
al mio comando	at my command
tutto qui sta.	everything's ready.
V'è la risorsa	Then there are "extras",

poi del mestiere,
colla donnetta,
col cavaliere...
La la ran la...la...la.
Ah, che bel vivere,
che bel piacere,
per un barbiere
di qualità.
Tutti mi chiedono,
tutti mi vogliono,
donne, ragazzi,
vecchi, fanciulle.
Qua la parrucca,
presto la barba,
qua la sanguigna,
presto il biglietto.
Tutti mi chiedono,
tutti mi vogliono.
Qua la parrucca,
presto la barba,
presto il biglietto.
Ehi, Figaro, Figaro, Figaro, ecc.
Ahimè! Che furia!
Ahimè! che folla!
Uno alla volta,
per carità.
Ehi, Figaro; son qua!
Figaro qua, Figaro là,
Figaro su, Figaro giù.
Pronto, prontissimo
son come il fulmine,
sono il factotum della città.
Ah, bravo, Figaro,
bravo, bravissimo,
A te la fortuna
non mancherà.
La la ran la, ecc.

part of my trade,
business for ladies
and cavaliers...
La la ran la...la...la.
Ah, what a merry life,
what gay pleasures,
for a barber
of quality.
All call for me,
all want me,
ladies and children,
old men and maidens.
I need a wig,
I want a shave,
leeches to bleed me,
here, take this note.
All call for me,
all want me,
I need a wig,
I want a shave,
here, take this note.
Ho, Figaro, Figaro, Figaro, etc.
Heavens! What a commotion!
Heavens! What a crowd!
One at a time,
for pity's sake.
Ho, Figaro! I am here!
Figaro here, Figaro there,
Figaro up, Figaro down.
Quicker and quicker
I go like greased lightning,
make way for the factotum of the city.
Ah, bravo, Figaro,
bravo, bravissimo,
On you good fortune
will always smile.
La la ran la, etc.

Sono il factotum della città.
Ah, che bella vita!
Faticar poco, divertirsi assai,
e in tasca sempre aver
qualche doblone,
gran frutto della mia riputazione.
Ecco qua; senza Figaro
non si accasa in Siviglia una ragazza;
a me la vedovella ricorre pel marito;
io, colla scusa del pettine di giorno,
della chitarra col favor la notte,
a tutti onestamente, non fo per dir,
m'adatto a far piacere.
Oh, che vita, oh, che mestiere!

I am the factotum of the city.
Ah! ah! what a happy life!
little fatigue, and much amusement,
always with some money in my pocket,
noble fruition of my reputation.
So it is: without Figaro
not a girl in Seville can marry;
to me come the little widows
for a husband; with the excuse
of my comb by day,
of my guitar by night,
to all, and I say it without boasting,
I honestly give service.
Oh, what a life, what a trade!

(Figaro goes up right on the way to his shop; the Count comes out of hiding.)

Orsù, presto a bottega -

Now, away to the shop -

CONTE
(È desso, oppur m'inganno?)

COUNT
(It is he, am I mistaken?)

FIGARO
(Chi sarà mai costui?)

FIGARO
(Who may this be?)

CONTE
(Oh, è lui senz'altro!) Figaro...

COUNT
(Oh! it's certainly he!) Figaro...

FIGARO
Mio padrone...Oh! Chi veggo!
Eccellenza...

FIGARO
My master... oh! Whom do I see?
Your Excellency...

CONTE
Zitto, zitto! Prudenza!
Qui non son conosciuto,
né vo' farmi conoscere.
Per questo ho le mie gran ragioni.

COUNT
Hush! Be prudent!
I am not known here,
nor do I wish to be.
I have the best of reasons.

FIGARO
Intendo, intendo, la lascio in libertà.

CONTE
No...

FIGARO
Che serve?

CONTE
No, dico, resta qua.
Forse ai disegni miei
 non giungi inopportuno.
Ma cospetto! dimmi un po', buona lana,
come ti trovo qua, poter del mondo!
Ti veggo grasso e tondo...

FIGARO
La miseria, signore!

CONTE
Ah, birbo!

FIGARO
Grazie.

CONTE
Hai messo ancor giudizio?

FIGARO
Oh! e come! Ed ella, come in Siviglia?

CONTE
Or te lo spiego. Al Prado
vidi un fior di bellezza, una fanciulla,
figlia d'un certo medico barbogio
che qua da pochi dì s'è stabilito;

FIGARO
I understand, I'll leave you alone.

COUNT
No...

FIGARO
What can I do?

COUNT
No, I tell you, stay here.
Perhaps for my purpose
you've come at the right time.
But tell me, you wily rascal,
how did you come here, Lord Almighty!
I see you're fat and fine...

FIGARO
Hard times brought me, sir!

COUNT
What a scoundrel!

FIGARO
Thank you.

COUNT
Are you behaving yourself?

FIGARO
And how! And you, why in Seville?

COUNT
I will explain. On the Prado
I beheld a flower of beauty, a maiden,
the daughter of a silly old physician,
who recently established himself here;

io di questa invaghito,
lasciai patria e parenti;
e qua men venni,
e qui la notte ed il giorno
passo girando a quei balconi intorno.

FIGARO
A quei balconi? Un medico?
Ah, cospetto! siete ben fortunato;
sui maccheroni, il cacio v'è cascato.

CONTE
Come?

FIGARO
Certo. Là dentro io son
barbiere, parrucchier, chirurgo.
Botanico, spezial, veterinario...
Insomma, il faccendier di casa.

CONTE
Oh, che sorte!

FIGARO
Non basta. La ragazza figlia
non è del medico.
È soltanto la sua pupilla.

CONTE
Oh, che consolazione!

FIGARO
Perciò...zitto...

CONTE
Cos'è?

enamoured of this damsel,
I left home and country;
and here I came,
and here, night and day,
I watch and wander near this balcony.

FIGARO
Near this balcony? A physician?
You are very fortunate;
the cheese fell right on the macaroni!

COUNT
Explain!

FIGARO
Certainly. In this house
I am barber, surgeon,
botanist, apothecary, veterinary...
In other words, I run the house.

COUNT
Oh, what luck!

FIGARO
But this is not all. The girl is not
the daughter of the physician.
She is only his ward.

COUNT
Oh, what a consolation!

FIGARO
But...hush...

COUNT
What is it?

FIGARO
S'apre il balcone...

(Rosina opens the balcony shutters, a piece of paper in her hand.)

ROSINA
Non è venuto ancora. Forse...

CONTE
Oh, mia vita! mio nume! mio tesoro! vi veggo alfine,
alfine...

ROSINA
Oh, che vergogna! vorrei dargli il biglietto...

BARTOLO *(comparendo sul balcone)*
Ebben, ragazza? Il tempo è buono. Cos'è quella carta?

ROSINA
Niente, niente, signore: son le parole del-
l'aria
dell'Inutil precauzione.

CONTE
Ma brava...dell'Inutil precauzione!

FIGARO
Che furba!

BARTOLO
Cos'è questa Inutil precauzione?

ROSINA
Oh, bella!

FIGARO
The balcony window opens...

ROSINA
He hasn't come yet. Maybe...

COUNT
Oh, my life! My goddess! My treasure! I see you at last, at
last...

ROSINA
Oh, what a shame! I'd like to give him the letter...

BARTOLO *(appearing on the balcony)*
Well, girl? The weather's fine. What's that paper?

ROSINA
Nothing at all, sir: just the words of the aria from the
Futile Precaution.

COUNT
Clever girl...the Futile Precaution?

FIGARO
Crafty minx!

BARTOLO
What is this Futile Precaution?

ROSINA
Well, really!

è il titolo del nuovo dramma in musica.

BARTOLO
Un dramma! Bella cosa! Sarà al solito un dramma semi-
serio, un lungo, malinconico, noioso, poet-
ico strambotto.
Barbaro gusto! secolo corrotto!

ROSINA (*lasciando cadere il foglio di carta*)
Oh, me meschina! L'aria m'è caduta.
Raccoglietela presto.

BARTOLO
Vado, vado.

(Bartolo goes inside, Rosina calls to the Count.)

ROSINA
Ps...ps...

CONTE
Ho inteso -

(He picks up the paper.)

ROSINA
Presto.

CONTE
Non temete.

BARTOLO
Son qua. Dov'è?

ROSINA
Ah, il vento l'ha portata via. Guardate.

it's the name of the new opera.

BARTOLO
An opera! Fine thing! As usual it will be a semi-serious
play, a long, melancholy, boring, poetic rig-
marole. In the
worst taste! What a corrupt age!

ROSINA (*dropping the paper*)
Oh, poor me! it's fallen.
Go and get it at once.

BARTOLO
I'm going, I'm going.

ROSINA
Pst...Pst!

COUNT
I understand -

ROSINA
Quickly.

COUNT
Never fear.

BARTOLO
I'm here. Where is it?

ROSINA
Oh, the wind's blown it away. Look.

BARTOLO
Io non la veggo.
Eh, signorina, non vorrei...
(Cospetto! costei m'avesse preso!...)
In casa, in casa, animo, su.
A chi dico? In casa, presto.

BARTOLO
I can't see it.
Now, young lady, I don't want...
(Heavens! she might have tricked me!)...
Go back into the house, be quick about it.
Must I tell you twice? Back into the house,
at once.

ROSINA
Vado, vado. Che furia!

ROSINA
I'm going, I'm going. What a fuss!

BARTOLO
Quel balcone voglio far murare...
Dentro, dico.

BARTOLO
I'll have that balcony walled up...
Go inside, I say.

ROSINA
Ah, che vita da crepare!

ROSINA
Oh, what an awful life!

(Bartolo goes back into the house; Rosina goes inside and closes the balcony shutters.)

CONTE
Povera disgraziata! Il suo stato infelice sempre più
m'interessa.

COUNT
Poor, unhappy girl! Her sad plight interests me more and
more.

FIGARO
Presto, presto: vediamo cosa scrive.

FIGARO
Quickly: let's see what she's written.

CONTE
Appunto. Leggi.

COUNT
Exactly. Read it.

(Figaro reads Rosina's letter to the Count.)

FIGARO
"Le vostre assidue premure hanno eccitata la mia

FIGARO
"Your constant attentions have aroused my curiosity. My

curiosità. Il mio tutore è per uscir di casa;
appena si
sarà allontanato, procurate con qualche
mezzo ingegnoso
d'indicarmi il vostro nome, il vostro stato e
le vostre
intenzioni. Io non posso giammai compar-
ire al balcone,
senza l'indivisibile compagnia del mio
tiranno. Siate però certo, che tutto è dis-
posta a fare, per rompere le
sue catene, la sventurata Rosina..."

CONTE
Sì, sì, le romperà.
Su, dimmi un poco:
che razza d'uomo
è questo suo tutore?

FIGARO
Un vecchio indemoniato,
avaro, sospettoso, brontolone,
avrà cent'anni indosso
e vuol fare il galante:
indovinate!
Per mangiare a Rosina tutta l'eredità
s'è fitto in capo di volerla sposare.
Aiuto!

CONTE
Che?

FIGARO
S'apre la porta.

guardian is just leaving; as soon as he's
gone, find some
ingenious means to tell me your name,
your rank and your
intentions. I can never appear on the balcony except in the
strict company of my tyrant. Rest assured,
however, that
unfortunate Rosina is prepared to do anything to break her
chains."

COUNT
Yes, yes, she shall break them.
Come, tell me:
what kind of man
is this guardian of hers?

FIGARO
He's an old devil,
miserly, suspicious, crabbed,
he must be a hundred
but wants to play the gallant:
and just imagine,
so as to enjoy Rosina's entire legacy
he's taken it into his head to marry her.
Help!

COUNT
What is it?

FIGARO
The door's opening.

(The Count and Figaro run away. The door opens and Bartolo comes out of the house.)

BARTOLO
Fra momenti io torno.
Non aprite a nessuno.
Se Don Basilio venisse a ricercarmi,
che m'aspetti.

(He locks the door from the outside.)

Le mie nozze con lei meglio è affrettare.

(He goes off.)

Sì, dentr'oggi finir vo' quest'affare.

CONTE
Dentr'oggi le sue nozze con Rosina!
Ah, vecchio rimbambito!
Ma dimmi or tu, chi è questo Don Basilio?

FIGARO
È un solenne imbroglion di matrimoni,
un collo torto, un vero disperato,
sempre senza un quattrino...
già, è maestro di musica,
insegna alla ragazza.

CONTE
Bene, tutto giova saper.

FIGARO
Ora pensate della bella Rosina
a soddisfar le brame.

CONTE
Il nome mio non le vo' dir
né il grado:

BARTOLO
I shall return in a few minutes.
Don't let anyone in. If Don Basilio
should come to inquire for me,
let him wait.

I wish to hasten my marriage with her.

Yes, this day. I am going to conclude this affair.

COUNT
This very day, his marriage with Rosina!
Oh, the foolish old dotard!
But tell me, who is this Don Basilio?

FIGARO
A famous, intriguing matchmaker,
a hypocrite, a good-for-nothing,
with never a penny in his pocket...
He has lately turned music-maker,
and teaches this girl.

COUNT
Well, that's good to know.

FIGARO
Now you must think how to tell the pretty
Rosina what she wants to know.

COUNT
I don't want to tell her my name
or my rank:

assicurarmi vo' pria ch'ella ami me,
me solo al mondo,
non le ricchezze e i titoli
del Conte Almaviva. Ah! tu potresti...

FIGARO
Io? no, signor;
voi stesso dovete...

CONTE
Io stesso? E come?

FIGARO
Zi...zitto. Eccoci a tiro, osservate:
per bacco, non mi sbaglio.
Dietro la gelosia sta la ragazza:
presto, presto all'assalto, niun ci vede.
In una canzonetta, così alla buona
il tutto spiegatele, signor.

CONTE
Una canzone?

FIGARO
Certo. Ecco la chitarra.
Presto, andiamo.

CONTE
Ma io...

FIGARO
Oh, che pazienza!

CONTE
Ebben, proviamo...
Se il mio nome saper voi bramate,
dal mio labbro il mio nome ascoltate.

I first want to be sure that she loves me
and me alone in all the world,
not the wealth and titles
of Count Almaviva. Ah, you could...

FIGARO
Me? My lord;
you yourself should...

COUNT
I? But how?

FIGARO
Shhh! What a stroke of luck!
By Jove, I'm not mistaken.
The girl's there behind the shutter.
Quick, quick, into action, no one's look-
ing. With a simple little song
you can explain it all to her, sir.

COUNT
A song?

FIGARO
Certainly. Here is my guitar.
Come, let's start.

COUNT
But I...

FIGARO
Heaven give me patience!

COUNT
Well, we'll try...
If you want to know my name,
listen to the song I sing.

Io son Lindoro,
che fido v'adoro,
che sposa vi bramo,
che a nome vi chiamo,
di voi sempre parlando così
dall'aurora al tramonto del dì.

I am called Lindoro,
who faithfully adores you,
who wishes to marry you,
your name is on my lips,
and you are in my thoughts,
from early dawn till late at night.

(Rosina answers from behind the shutters.)

ROSINA
Segui, oh caro,
deh, segui così.

ROSINA
Continue, beloved,
continue to sing.

FIGARO
Sentite. Ah! che vi pare?

FIGARO
Listen! What could be better?

CONTE
Oh, me felice!

COUNT
What happiness!

FIGARO
Da bravo, a voi, seguite.

FIGARO
Bravo! Now continue.

CONTE
L'amoroso e sincero Lindoro
 non può darvi, mia cara, un tesoro.
Ricco non sono,
ma un core vi dono,
un'anima amante
che fida e costante
per voi sola sospira, così
dall'aurora al tramonto del dì.

COUNT
Sincere and enamoured Lindoro
cannot give you, my dear, a fortune.
Rich, I am not,
but heart I can give,
a loving spirit
which faithful and true,
for you only breathes,
from early dawn till late at night.

(Rosina answers again from inside.)

ROSINA
L'amorosa, sincera Rosina
del suo core Lindo...

ROSINA
Sincere and enamoured Rosina
her heart to Lin...

(She breaks off and leaves the balcony.)

CONTE
Oh, cielo!

FIGARO
Nella stanza convien dir che qualcuno
entrato sia. Ella si è ritirata.

CONTE
Ah, cospettone!
Io già deliro, avvampo!
Oh, ad ogni costo
vederla io voglio, vo' parlarle!
Ah, tu, tu mi devi aiutar.

FIGARO
Ih, ih, che furia!
Sì, sì, v'aiuterò.

CONTE
Da bravo! Entr'oggi vo' che tu
m'introduca in quella casa.
Dimmi, come farai?
Via, del tuo spirito
vediam qualche prodezza.

FIGARO
Del mio spirito!
Bene, vedrò...ma in oggi...

CONTE
Eh, via! T'intendo.
Va là, non dubitar;
di tue fatiche
largo compenso avrai.

COUNT
Oh, Heavens!

FIGARO
I imagine someone entered her room.
She has gone inside.

COUNT
Oh, damnation!
I am feverish, on fire!
At any cost
I must see her, speak to her!
You, you must help me.

FIGARO
Ha, ha, what a frenzy!
Yes, yes, I shall help you.

COUNT
Bravo! Before nightfall
you must get me into the house.
Tell me, how can you do it?
Come, let's see some feat
of your imagination.

FIGARO
Of my imagination!
Well, I shall see...but nowadays...

COUNT
Yes, yes! I understand.
Go ahead, don't worry;
your efforts
will be rewarded.

FIGARO
Davver?

CONTE
Parola.

FIGARO
Dunque oro a discrezione?

CONTE
Oro a bizzeffe!
Animo, via!

FIGARO
Truly?

COUNT
On my word.

FIGARO
Gold in abundance?

COUNT
To your heart's content.
Come, on your way.

disc no. 1/track 13 *All'idea di quel metallo* Figaro and the Count make a plan in the kind of sparkling duet that shows how vividly Rossini explores his characters by repeating, embellishing and contrasting basically simple musical material. Figaro begins earnestly, with a jaunty little tune that bristles with his happy determination to help the Count. A satisfied turn of melody follows **(00:48)**, suggesting that the two are definitely "on the same page" and still thinking. In the exchanges that follow, the two trade off the jaunty tune, with that satisfied-sounding melody suggesting their delight in their plans. But Figaro wonders **(3:08)**: what if the Count played a drunk? He explains **(03:43)** that Bartolo, perversely, would be more likely to trust a drunk. They agree: what a great idea! **(4:22)** The two almost part, until the count asks for directions to Figaro's shop. Figaro tells him, in a buoyant waltz-like melody **(05:25)**, where he find the shop; the barber's expression swells with pride. After briefly reassuring each of the terms of the deal, the Count relaunches the waltz melody **(06:45)**, as each of them expresses his own satisfaction and hope in counterpoint to the other. With typically Rossinian punctuation—the excited chattering in the orchestra **(07:42)**—the Count and Figaro celebrate their cunning.

FIGARO
Son pronto. Ah, non sapete
i simpatici effetti prodigiosi
che ad appagare il mio signor Lindoro

FIGARO
I'm ready. You cannot imagine
what a prodigious devotion
the sweet thought of gold

57

produce in me la dolce idea dell'oro.
All'idea di quel metallo
portentoso, onnipossente,
un vulcano la mia mente
già comincia a diventar, sì.

CONTE
Su, vediamo di quel metallo
qualche effetto sorprendente,
del vulcan della tua mente
qualche mostro singolar, sì.

FIGARO
Voi dovreste travestirvi...
per esempio...da soldato...

CONTE
Da soldato?

FIGARO
Sì, signore.

CONTE
Da soldato, e che si fa?

FIGARO
Oggi arriva un reggimento.

CONTE
Sì, è mio amico il colonnello.

FIGARO
Va benon!

CONTE
Eppoi?

makes me feel towards Lindoro.
At the idea of this metal
portentous, omnipotent,
a volcano within me
commences to erupt, yes.

COUNT
Come, let's see what effect
this metal will have on you,
some real demonstration
of this volcano within you, yes.

FIGARO
You should disguise yourself...
for instance...as a soldier...

COUNT
As a soldier?

FIGARO
Yes, sir.

COUNT
As a soldier, and for what purpose?

FIGARO
Today a regiment is expected here.

COUNT
Yes, the colonel is a friend of mine.

FIGARO
Excellent!

COUNT
And then?

FIGARO
Cospetto! Dell'alloggio col biglietto
quella porta s'aprirà.
Che ne dite, mio signore?
Non vi par, non l'ho trovata?
Che invenzione prelibata,
bella, bella in verità!

CONTE
Che invenzione prelibata,
bravo, bravo, in verità!

FIGARO
Piano, piano...un'altra idea!
Veda l'oro cosa fa!
Ubbriaco, mio signor, si fingerà.

CONTE
Ubbriaco?

FIGARO
Sì, signore.

CONTE
Ubbriaco? Ma perché?

FIGARO
Perché d'un ch'è poco in sé,
che dal vino casca già,
il tutor, credete a me,
il tutor si fiderà.

ASSIEME
Che invenzione prelibata,
bravo, bravo, in verità!

FIGARO
By means of a billet,
that door will soon open.
What say you to this, sir?
Don't you think I've hit it right?
Isn't it a fine idea,
happy thought, in very truth!

COUNT
Isn't it a fine idea,
happy thought, in very truth!

FIGARO
Softly, softly...another thought!
See the power of your gold!
You must pretend to be drunk.

COUNT
Drunk?

FIGARO
Even so, sir.

COUNT
Drunk? But why?

FIGARO
Because the guardian, believe me,
the guardian would less distrust
a man not quite himself,
but overcome with wine.

BOTH
Isn't it a fine idea,
happy thought, in very truth!

CONTE
Dunque?

FIGARO
All'opra.

CONTE
Andiamo.

FIGARO
Da bravo.

(They start to leave in opposite directions. The Count calls Figaro back.)

CONTE
Oh, il meglio mi scordavo.
Dimmi un po': la tua bottega,
per trovarti, dove sta?

FIGARO
La bottega?...Non si sbaglia...
guardi bene...eccola là...
Numero quindici, a mano manca,
quattro gradini, facciata bianca,
cinque parrucche nella vetrina,
sopra un cartello, "Pomata Fina",
mostra in azzurro alla moderna,
v'è per insegna una lanterna...
Là senza fallo mi troverà.

CONTE
Ho ben capito.

FIGARO
Or vada presto.

COUNT
Well, then?

FIGARO
To business.

COUNT
Let's go.

FIGARO
Bravo.

COUNT
...but the most important thing
I forgot to ask: tell me,
where do I find your shop?

FIGARO
My shop? you cannot mistake it...
look yonder...there it is...
number fifteen, on the left hand,
with four steps, a white front,
five wigs in the window,
on a placard, "Pomade Divine",
a show-glass, too, of the latest fashion,
and my sign is a lantern...
There, without fail you will find me.

COUNT
I understand.

FIGARO
You had better go now.

CONTE
Tu guarda bene...

FIGARO
Io penso al resto.

CONTE
Di te mi fido...

FIGARO
Colà l'attendo...

CONTE
Mio caro Figaro...

FIGARO
Intendo, intendo...

CONTE
Porterò meco...

FIGARO
La borsa piena.

CONTE
Sì, quel che vuoi,
ma il resto poi...

FIGARO
Oh, non si dubiti,
che bene andrà.

CONTE
Ah, che d'amore
la fiamma io sento,
nunzia di giubilo
e di contento!

COUNT
And you watch out...

FIGARO
I'll take care of everything.

COUNT
I have faith in you...

FIGARO
I shall wait for you yonder...

COUNT
My dear Figaro...

FIGARO
I understand, I understand...

COUNT
I will bring with me...

FIGARO
A purse well filled.

COUNT
Yes, all you want,
but do your part...

FIGARO
Oh, have no doubt,
all will go well.

COUNT
Oh, what a flame
of love divine,
of hope and joy
auspicious sign!

D'ardor insolito
quest'alma accende,
e di me stesso
maggior mi fa.
Ah, che d'amore, ecc.
Ecco propizia
che in sen mi scende
d'ardor insolito
quest'alma accende
e di me stesso
maggior mi fa.

FIGARO

Delle monete
il suon già sento,
l'oro già viene...
Eccolo qua.
Già viene l'oro,
viene l'argento,
in tasca scende...
Eccolo qua.
D'ardore insolito
quest'alma accende,
e di me stesso
maggior mi fa.

With fire unknown
my soul is burning,
and fills my spirit
with will to dare.
Oh, what a flame, etc.
Oh, glorious moment
which inspires my heart!
With fire unknown
my soul is burning,
and fills my spirit
with will to dare.

FIGARO

I almost can hear
the clinking coin,
gold is coming...
already it's here.
Gold is coming,
silver is coming,
filling the pockets...
already it's here.
With fire unknown
my soul is burning,
and fills my spirit
with will to dare.

(They leave.)

SCENE 2

A COURTYARD IN BARTOLO'S HOUSE

disc no. 1/track 14 *Una voce poco fa* The orchestra almost giggles with delight as it introduces Rosina. She sings to herself **(00:32)**, in gently excited little phrases suggesting her delight in being love. She can barely contain herself when she thinks of Lindoro **(01:35)**, her passion mingling with concern about Bartolo's interference in bursts of coloratura. However, the orchestra informs us as the second part of the aria begins **(02:20)**...Rosina is not to be underestimated when crossed. She asserts what a sweet girl she is (02:45) until she delivers a very pointed "but" on the Italian word "ma" **(03:12)**. Her ever-bolder flights of coloratura remind us that she has plenty of tricks up her sleeve, as she repeats and emphasizes (in decorated phrases that reach higher and higher) her determination to be with Lindoro.

ROSINA *(con una lettera in mano)*
Una voce poco fa
qui nel cor mi risuonò.
Il mio cor ferito è già
e Lindoro fu che il piagò.
Sì, Lindoro mio sarà,
lo giurai, la vincerò.
Il tutor ricuserà,
io l'ingegno aguzzerò,
alla fin s'accheterà,
e contenta io resterò.
Sì, Lindoro ecc.
Io sono docile,
son rispettosa,
sono obbediente,
dolce, amorosa,
mi lascio reggere,
mi fo guidar.
Ma se mi toccano
dov'è il mio debole,
sarò una vipera, sarò,
e cento trappole
prima di cedere farò giocar.
Io sono docile, ecc.
Sì, sì, la vincerò.
Potessi almeno
mandargli questa lettera.
Ma come? Di nessun qui mi fido.
Il tutore ha cent'occhi...

ROSINA *(with a letter in her hand)*
The voice I heard just now
has thrilled my very heart.
My heart already is pierced
and it was Lindoro who hurled the dart.
Yes, Lindoro shall be mine,
I've sworn it, I'll succeed.
My guardian won't consent,
but I will sharpen my wits,
and at last, he will relent,
and I shall be content.
Yes, Lindoro etc.
I am docile,
I am respectful,
I am obedient,
sweet and loving.
I can be ruled,
I can be guided.
But if crossed in love,
I can be a viper,
and a hundred tricks
I shall play
before they have their way.
I am docile, etc.
Yes, yes, I shall conquer.
If I could only
send him this letter.
But how? There is none I can trust.
My guardian has a hundred eyes...

Basta…basta…sigilliamola intanto.
Con Figaro, il barbier, dalla finestra
discorrer l'ho veduto più d'un'ora.
Figaro è un galantuomo,
un giovin di buon core…
Chi sa ch'ei non protegga
il nostro amore!

Well, well…meanwhile I'll seal it.
From my window I saw him, for an hour,
talking with Figaro, the barber.
Figaro is an honest fellow,
a good-hearted soul…
who knows, he may be the one
to protect our love!

(Figaro enters from upstage, Rosina hides her letter.)

FIGARO
Oh, buon dì, signorina.

FIGARO
Good day, signorina.

ROSINA
Buon giorno, signor Figaro.

ROSINA
Good day, signor Figaro.

FIGARO
Ebbene? Che si fa?

FIGARO
Well? how are you?

ROSINA
Si muor di noia.

ROSINA
I am dying of boredom.

FIGARO
Oh, diavolo! Possibile!
Una ragazza bella e spiritosa…

FIGARO
The deuce! Is that possible!
A lovely girl, full of spirits…

ROSINA
Ah! Ah! Mi fate ridere!
Che mi serve lo spirito,
che giova la bellezza,
se chiusa sempre sto
fra quattro mura
che mi par d'esser
 proprio in sepoltura?

ROSINA
Ah! you make me laugh!
Of what use is my spirit,
what good is my beauty,
if I am always shut up
between four walls
and feel as if I am living
inside a sepulchre?

FIGARO
In sepoltura? Oibò!…

FIGARO
A sepulchre? Heavens!…

Sentite, io voglio...

But I must talk with you...

(The street door is being opened.)

ROSINA
Ecco il tutor.

ROSINA
My guardian is coming.

FIGARO
Davvero?

FIGARO
Truly?

ROSINA
Certo, certo. È il suo passo.

ROSINA
Definitely. I know his footstep.

FIGARO *(ritirandosi)*
Salva, salva! Fra poco ci rivedremo!
Ho da dirvi qualche cosa.

FIGARO *(retreating upstage)*
Adieu, adieu! I will see you soon again.
I have something to tell you.

ROSINA
E ancor io, signor Figaro.

ROSINA
And I too, signor Figaro.

FIGARO
Bravissima. Vado.

FIGARO
Bravissima. I go.

(He hides himself.)

ROSINA
Quanto è garbato!

ROSINA
What a nice fellow he is!

(Bartolo enters from the street.)

BARTOLO
Ah, disgraziato Figaro!
Ah, indegno, ah, maledetto,
ah, scellerato!

BARTOLO
Oh, that menace of a Figaro!
What a rascal, what a villain,
what a scoundrel!

ROSINA
(Ecco qua. Sempre grida.)

ROSINA
(He's off again. Always shouting.)

BARTOLO
Ma si può dar di peggio!
Un ospedale ha fatto
di tutta la famiglia
a forza d'oppio, sangue e stranutiglia.
Signorina, il barbiere...lo vedeste?

ROSINA
Perché?

BARTOLO
Perché lo vo' sapere!

ROSINA
Forse anch'egli v'adombra?

BARTOLO
E perché no?

ROSINA
Ebben, ve lo dirò.
Sì, l'ho veduto, gli ho parlato,
mi piace, m'è simpatico il suo discorso,

il suo gioviale aspetto.
(Crepa di rabbia, vecchio maledetto!)

(Rosina goes up to her room.)

BARTOLO
Vedete che grazietta!
Più l'amo
e più mi sprezza la briccona.
Certo, certo è il barbiere
che la mette in malizia.
Chi sa cosa le ha detto! Chi sa! Or lo saprò.

BARTOLO
They don't come any worse!
With opium, blood and sneezing powder
he has made a hospital
of the whole household.
Signorina, the barber...have you seen him?

ROSINA
Why?

BARTOLO
Why? Because I want to know!

ROSINA
Has he, too, put you in a rage?

BARTOLO
And why not?

ROSINA
Alright, I shall tell you.
Yes, I saw him, I spoke with him,
I like him, I enjoy talking with him,

I find him handsome.
(Choke on that, wicked old man!)

BARTOLO
What a charming little miss!
The more I love her,
the more she disdains me.
There is no doubt, it is the barber
who has put her up to this.
Hey! Berta! Ambrogio! Who knows what

Ehi, Berta!
Ambrogio!

he's told her. I
wonder. Now I'll find out.

(Berta enters, sneezing; Ambrogio also enters, yawning.)

BERTA
Eccì...

BERTA
A-tishoo...

AMBROGIO
Ah ah! Che comanda?

AMBROGIO
Aah...aah! what are your orders?

BARTOLO
Il barbiere parlato ha con Rosina?

BARTOLO
Has the barber been talking to Rosina?

BERTA
Eccì...

BERTA
A-tishoo...

BARTOLO
Rispondi almen tu, babbuino.

BARTOLO
You answer, at least, you oaf.

AMBROGIO
Ah ah!

AMBROGIO
Aah...aah!

BARTOLO
Che pazienza!

BARTOLO
Oh, for patience!

AMBROGIO
Ah ah!...che sonno!

AMBROGIO
Aah...aah! How sleepy I am!

BARTOLO
Ebben!

BARTOLO
Well?

BERTA
Venne, ma io...

BERTA
He came, but I...

BARTOLO
Rosina...?

BARTOLO
And Rosina...?

AMBROGIO
Ah ah!

BERTA
Eccì...

BARTOLO
Che serve! eccoli qua, son mezzo morti.
Andate.

AMBROGIO
Ah ah!

BERTA
Eccì...

BARTOLO
Eh, il diavolo che vi porti!
Ah! Barbiere d'inferno...
Tu me la pagherai!

AMBROGIO
Aah...aah!

BERTA
A-tishoo...

BARTOLO
What servants! Here they are, half dead.
Go now!

AMBROGIO
Aah...aah!

BERTA
A-tishoo...

BARTOLO
Oh, the devil take the pair of you!
Oh! Devil of a barber...
You shall pay for this!

(chases both of them away. Basilio enters.)

Qua, Don Basilio, giungete a tempo.
Oh! io voglio per forza o per amor
dentro dimani sposar la mia Rosina.
Avete inteso?

DON BASILIO
Eh, voi dite benissimo,
e appunto io qui veniva ad avvisarvi.
Ma segretezza...
È giunto il Conte Almaviva.

BARTOLO
Chi? L'incognito amante della Rosina?

Don Basilio, you come at the right time.
By force or by love,
by tomorrow I must marry Rosina.
Is that clear?

DON BASILIO
Eh, you speak wisely,
and it is for that very reason I have come.
But keep this secret...
Count Almaviva has arrived.

BARTOLO
Who? The unknown lover of Rosina?

DON BASILIO
Appunto quello.

BARTOLO
Oh, diavolo! Ah! Qui ci vuol rimedio.

DON BASILIO
Certo. Ma alla sordina.

BARTOLO
Sarebbe a dir?

DON BASILIO
Così, con buona grazia,
bisogna principiare
a inventar qualche favola
che al pubblico lo metta in mala vista,
che comparir lo faccia
un uomo infame, un'anima perduta...
Io, io vi servirò;
fra quattro giorni, credete a me,
Basilio ve lo giura,
noi lo farem sloggiar
da queste mura.

BARTOLO
E voi credete?

DON BASILIO
Oh, certo! È il mio sistema,
e non sbaglia.

BARTOLO
E vorreste? Ma...una calunnia...

DON BASILIO
Ah, dunque la calunnia cos'è!

DON BASILIO
The very same.

BARTOLO
Oh, the devil! Something must be done.

DON BASILIO
Certainly. But very hush-hush.

BARTOLO
That is to say?

DON BASILIO
Just this, that plausibly,
we must begin
to invent a story
which will put him in a bad light
with the public, making him seem
a man of infamy, a doomed soul...
I shall attend to this;
within four days,
on the word of Basilio,
he'll be thrown out
of this town.

BARTOLO
Do you really think so?

DON BASILIO
Without a doubt! I have my own system,
and it is foolproof.

BARTOLO
And you would dare? But...calumny...

DON BASILIO
Ah, what is calumny!

Voi non sapete?

Don't you know?

BARTOLO
No, davvero.

BARTOLO
In truth, I do not.

disc no. 1 track 18 *La calunnia è un venticello* A stately melody announces Don Basilio's sermon-like explanation of calumny and its infectious nature. Accompanied by the kind of "busy" Rossini musical figure that should be familiar by now (00:56), he describes the way it spreads, with the music swelling and intensifying— another trademark Rossini crescendo—into an explosion. Catching his breath after this outburst (02:40), a new melody allows Basilio to smugly make (and reinforce) his point: calumny can kill a poor soul.

DON BASILIO
No? Uditemi e tacete.
La calunnia è un venticello
un'auretta assai gentile
che insensibile, sottile,
leggermente, dolcemente,
incomincia a sussurrar.
Piano, piano, terra terra,
sottovoce, sibilando,
va scorrendo, va ronzando.
Nell'orecchie della gente,
s'introduce destramente
e le teste ed i cervelli
fa stordire e fa gonfiar.
Dalla bocca fuori uscendo
lo schiamazzo va crescendo,
prende forza a poco a poco,
vola già di loco in loco,
sembra il tuono, la tempesta
che nel sen della foresta
va fischiando, brontolando,
e ti fa d'orror gelar.
Alla fin trabocca e scoppia,

DON BASILIO
No? Then hear and be silent.
Calumny is a little breeze,
a gentle zephyr
which insensibly, subtly,
lightly and sweetly,
commences to whisper.
Softly, softly, here and there,
sottovoce, sibilant,
it goes gliding, it goes rambling.
In the ears of the people,
it penetrates slyly
and the head and the brains
it stuns and it swells.
From the mouth re-emerging
the noise grows crescendo,
gathers force little by little,
runs its course from place to place,
seems like the thunder of the tempest
which from the depths of the forest
comes whistling, muttering,
freezing everyone in horror.
Finally with crack and crash,

si propaga, si raddoppia,
e produce un'esplosione
come un colpo di cannone,
un tremuoto, un temporale,
che fa l'aria rimbombar.
E il meschino calunniato,
avvilito, calpestato,
sotto il pubblico flagello,
 per gran sorte va a crepar.
Ah! Che ne dite?

BARTOLO
Eh! Sarà ver, ma intanto si perde tempo
e qui stringe il bisogno.
No, vo' fare a modo mio.
In mia camera andiam.
Voglio che insieme il contratto di nozze
ora stendiamo. Quando sarà mia moglie,

(moving off to his room)

da questi zerbinotti innamorati
metterla in salvo sarà pensier mio.

DON BASILIO *(seguendolo)*
(Vengan denari,
al resto son qua io.)

(Figaro, who has been hiding, comes forward.)

FIGARO
Ma bravi! Ma benone! Ho inteso tutto.
Evviva il buon Dottore! Povero babbuino!
Tua sposa? Eh, via!
Pulisciti il bocchino!

it spreads afield, its force redoubled,
and produces an explosion
like the outburst of a cannon,
an earthquake, a whirlwind,
which makes the air resound.
And the poor slandered wretch,
vilified, trampled down,
sunk beneath the public lash,
by good fortune,
falls to death.
Now what do you say?

BARTOLO
Eh! that may be true, but meanwhile
we are wasting valuable time.
No, I want to do things my own way.
Let's go into my room.
Together the marriage contract
we must prepare. When she is my wife,

I shall know very well
how to keep off these lovesick dandies.

DON BASILIO *(following him)*
(If there is money to make,
I am always on hand.)

FIGARO
Bravo! all goes well! I heard everything.
Hurrah for the good Doctor! Poor idiot!
Your wife? Come, come!
Don't make me laugh!

Or che stanno là chiusi
  procuriam di parlare alla ragazza...

While they are shut up in that room
I shall try to talk to the girl...

(Rosina comes down from her room.)

Eccola appunto.

But here she is.

ROSINA
Ebbene, signor Figaro?

ROSINA
Well, signor Figaro?

FIGARO
Gran cose, signorina.

FIGARO
Great things are happening, signorina.

ROSINA
Sì, davvero?

ROSINA
Indeed?

FIGARO
Mangerem dei confetti.

FIGARO
We shall eat wedding-cake soon.

ROSINA
Come sarebbe a dir?

ROSINA
What do you mean?

FIGARO
Sarebbe a dire
che il vostro bel tutore ha stabilito
esser dentro doman vostro marito.

FIGARO
I mean to say
that this fine guardian of yours
plans to be your husband by tomorrow.

ROSINA
Eh, via!

ROSINA
What nonsense!

FIGARO
Oh, ve lo giuro.
A stender il contratto
col maestro di musica
là dentro s'è serrato.

FIGARO
Oh, I swear it.
He has locked himself
in that room with your music-master
to draw up the contract.

ROSINA
Sì? Oh, l'ha sbagliata affè!
Povero sciocco!
L'avrà da far con me...
Ma dite, signor Figaro,
voi poco fa sotto le mie finestre
parlavate a un signore?

FIGARO

(moving away from Rosina, and making up a story)

Ah, un mio cugino.
Un bravo giovinotto,
buona testa, ottimo cor.
Qui venne i suoi studi a compire
e il poverin cerca di far fortuna.

ROSINA
Fortuna? Eh, la farà.

FIGARO
Oh, ne dubito assai.
In confidenza, ha un gran difetto addosso.

ROSINA
Un gran difetto?

FIGARO
Ah, grande. È innamorato morto.

ROSINA
Sì, davvero? Quel giovine, vedete,
m'interessa moltissimo.

FIGARO
Per bacco!

ROSINA
Yes? Well, he is much mistaken!
Poor fool!
He has me to deal with...
but tell me, signor Figaro,
a little while ago under my window
were you talking with a gentleman?

FIGARO

Yes, with my cousin.
A fine young man,
with a good head and a warm heart.
Poor fellow, he has come here
to finish his studies and to seek his fortune.

ROSINA
A fortune? Oh, he'll make it.

FIGARO
I doubt it.
Confidentially he has one great fault.

ROSINA
A great fault?

FIGARO
Yes, a great one. He is dying of love.

ROSINA
Really? That young man, you know,
interests me very much.

FIGARO
Good Lord!

ROSINA
Non ci credete?

FIGARO
Oh, sì!

ROSINA
E la sua bella, dite,
abita lontano?

FIGARO
Oh, no! Cioè...qui...due passi...

ROSINA
Ma è bella?

FIGARO
Oh, bella assai!
Eccovi il suo ritratto in due parole:
grassotta, genialotta,
capello nero, guancia porporina,
occhio che parla, mano che innamora.

ROSINA
E il nome?

FIGARO
Ah, il nome ancora! Il nome,
che bel nome! Si chiama...

ROSINA
Ebben? Si chiama?

FIGARO
Poverina!...
Si chiama R...O...Ro...
S...I...si....Rosi...

ROSINA
Don't you believe it?

FIGARO
Oh, yes!

ROSINA
And tell me, his beloved,
does she live far away?

FIGARO
Oh, no! That is...here...two steps...

ROSINA
But is she pretty?

FIGARO
Oh, pretty enough!
I can give you her picture in two words:
deliciously plump, high-spirited,
black hair, rosy cheeks,
sparkling eyes, enchanting hands.

ROSINA
And her name?

FIGARO
And her name too! Her name,
what a lovely name! She is called...

ROSINA
Well, what is she called?

FIGARO
Poor little dear!...
She is called R...O...Ro...
S...I...si...Rosi...

FIGARO E ROSINA
N...A...na...
Rosina!

FIGARO AND ROSINA
...N...A...na...
Rosina!

disc no. 1/track 21 *Dunque io son* Learning that she is indeed the beloved of Lindoro, Rosina stutters her delight, though volleys of coloratura give her away: she already knows. Figaro responds **(00:46)**, in wry echoes of the melody and coloratura Rosina has just sung. The conversational exchanges that follow show Rossini's gift for writing witty musical chitchat. The melodic material is varied only slightly, often in the musical elaborations that reflect the point being made in the text. Their excitement bubbles up in another Rossini crescendo **(03:38)**, which (also typically) pulls back with a second thought, before hurtling to a brilliant conclusion.

ROSINA
Dunque io son...tu non m'inganni?
Dunque io son la fortunata!
(Già me l'ero immaginata,
lo sapevo pria di te.)

FIGARO
Di Lindoro il vago oggetto
siete voi, bella Rosina.
(Oh, che volpe sopraffina!
Ma l'avrà da far con me.)

ROSINA
Senti, senti, ma a Lindoro
per parlar come si fa?

FIGARO
Zitto, zitto, qui Lindoro
per parlarvi ora sarà.

ROSINA
Per parlarmi? Bravo! Bravo!
Venga pur, ma con prudenza,

ROSINA
Then it is I....You are not mocking me?
Then I am the fortunate girl!
(But I had already guessed it,
I knew it all along.)

FIGARO
You are, sweet Rosina,
of Lindoro's love, the object.
(Oh, what a cunning little fox!
But she'll have to deal with me.)

ROSINA
But tell me, to Lindoro
how shall I contrive to speak?

FIGARO
Patience, patience, and Lindoro
soon your presence here will seek.

ROSINA
To speak to me? Bravo! Bravo!
Let him come, but with caution,

io già moro d'impazienza!
Ma che tarda? Cosa fa?

FIGARO
Egli attende qualche segno,
poverin, del vostro affetto;
sol due righe di biglietto
gli mandate e qui verrà.
Che ne dite?

ROSINA
Non vorrei...

FIGARO
Su, coraggio.

ROSINA
Non saprei...

FIGARO
Sol due righe...

ROSINA
Mi vergogno.

FIGARO
Ma di che? Ma di che? Si sa!
Presto, presto, qua il biglietto.

ROSINA
Un biglietto?...Eccolo qua.

(She takes a letter from her bosom and gives it to him.)

FIGARO
(Già era scritto...Ve' che bestia!
Il maestro faccio a lei!)

meanwhile I am dying of impatience!
Why is he delayed? What is he doing?

FIGARO
He is awaiting some sign,
poor man, of your affection;
send him but two lines
and you will see him here.
What do you say to this?

ROSINA
I shouldn't...

FIGARO
Come, courage.

ROSINA
I don't know...

FIGARO
Only two lines...

ROSINA
I am too shy.

FIGARO
But why? But why?
Quickly, quickly, give me a note.

ROSINA
A note?...Here it is.

FIGARO
(Already written...what a fool!
She could give me a lesson or two!)

ROSINA
Fortunati affetti miei,
io comincio a respirar.

FIGARO
(Ah, che in cattedra costei
di malizia può dettar.)

ROSINA
Ah, tu solo, amor, tu sei
che mi devi consolar.

FIGARO
(Donne, donne, eterni dei,
chi v'arriva a indovinar?)

ROSINA
Ah, tu solo, amor, tu sei
che mi devi consolar.

ROSINA
Senti, senti, ma Lindoro...

FIGARO
Qui verrà.
A momenti per parlarvi qui sarà.

ROSINA
Venga pur, ma con prudenza.

FIGARO
Zitto, zitto, qui verrà.

ROSINA
Fortunati affetti miei,
io comincio a respirar.
Ah, tu solo, amor, tu sei,

ROSINA
Fortune smiles on my love,
I can breathe once more.

FIGARO
(In cunning itself
she could be a professor.)

ROSINA
Oh, you alone, my love,
can console my heart.

FIGARO
(Women, women, eternal gods,
who can fathom their minds?)

ROSINA
Oh, you alone, my love,
can console my heart.

ROSINA
Tell me, but Lindoro...

FIGARO
Is on his way. In a few minutes
he'll be here to speak to you.

ROSINA
Let him come, but with caution.

FIGARO
Patience, patience, he'll be here.

ROSINA
Fortune smiles on my love,
I can breathe once more.
Oh, you alone, my love,

che mi devi consolar.

FIGARO
(Donne, donne, eterni dei,
chi v'arriva a indovinar?)

FIGARO
(Women, women, eternal gods,
who can fathom their minds?)

(Figaro leaves through the street door.)

ROSINA
Ora mi sento meglio,
questo Figaro è un bravo giovinotto.

ROSINA
Now I feel better.
That Figaro is a nice young man.

(Bartolo enters from his room.)

BARTOLO
Insomma, colle buone
potrei sapere dalla mia Rosina
che venne a far colui questa mattina?

BARTOLO
With fair words may I know
from my Rosina what brought
this fellow here this morning?

ROSINA
Figaro? Non so nulla.

ROSINA
Figaro? I know nothing.

BARTOLO
Ti parlò?

BARTOLO
He spoke to you?

ROSINA
Mi parlò.

ROSINA
He spoke to me.

BARTOLO
Che ti diceva?

BARTOLO
What was he telling you?

ROSINA
Oh, mi parlò di certe bagatelle...
Dei figurin di Francia,
del mal della sua figlia Marcellina.

ROSINA
Oh, he told me a hundred trifles...
Of the fashions in France,
of the illness of his daughter, Marcellina.

BARTOLO
Davvero?
Ed io scommetto...
che portò
la risposta al tuo biglietto.

ROSINA
Qual biglietto?

BARTOLO
Che serve!
L'arietta dell'Inutil precauzione
che ti cadde staman giù
dal balcone.
Vi fate rossa?
(Avessi indovinato!)
Che vuol dir questo dito
così sporco d'inchiostro?

ROSINA
Sporco? Oh! Nulla.
Io me l'avea scottato

e coll'inchiostro
or l'ho medicato.

BARTOLO
(Diavolo!)
E questi fogli...
or son cinque, eran sei.´

ROSINA
Que' fogli? È vero.
D'uno mi son servita a mandar
de' confetti a Marcellina.

BARTOLO
Indeed?
And I wager...
...that he brought
the reply to your note.

ROSINA
What note?

BARTOLO
Oh, what's the use?
The air from The Futile Precaution
which you dropped this morning
from the balcony.
You're blushing, eh?
(If only I'd guessed!)
What is the meaning
of your ink-stained finger?

ROSINA
Stained? Oh! nothing.
I burned myself

and I used the ink
as a medicine.

BARTOLO
The devil!
And these sheets of paper...
there are five now, there were six.

ROSINA
The note paper? You are right.
I used one to wrap the sweets
I sent to Marcellina.

BARTOLO
Bravissima!
E la penna
perché fu temperata?

ROSINA
(Maledetto!) La penna!
Per disegnare un fiore sul tamburo.

BARTOLO
Un fiore!

ROSINA
Un fiore.

BARTOLO
Un fiore! Ah! Fraschetta!

ROSINA
Davver.

BARTOLO
Zitto.

ROSINA
Credete...

BARTOLO
Basta così.

ROSINA
Signor...

BARTOLO
Non più...tacete.
A un dottor della mia sorte
queste scuse, signorina,

BARTOLO
Bravissima!
And the pen,
why was it sharpened?

ROSINA
(Heavens!) The pen!
To draw a flower to embroider.

BARTOLO
A flower!

ROSINA
A flower.

BARTOLO
A flower! Oh! you minx!

ROSINA
It is the truth.

BARTOLO
Silence.

ROSINA
Believe me...

BARTOLO
Enough of this.

ROSINA
Sir...

BARTOLO
No more...be quiet.
For a doctor of my standing
these excuses, signorina,

vi consiglio, mia carina,
un po' meglio a impostufar.
Meglio! Meglio! Meglio! Meglio!
I confetti alla ragazza!
Il ricamo sul tamburo!
Vi scottaste, eh via!
Ci vuol altro, figlia mia,
per potermi corbellar.
Altro! Altro! Altro! Altro!
Perché manca là quel foglio?
Vo' saper cotesto imbroglio.
Sono inutili le smorfie;
ferma là, non mi toccate.
Figlia mia, non lo sperate
ch'io mi lasci infinocchiar.
A un dottor della mia sorte
queste scuse, signorina,
vi consiglio, mia carina,
un po' meglio a impostufar.
Via carina, confessate.
Son disposto a perdonar.
Non parlate? Vi ostinate?
So ben io quel che ho da far.
Signorina, un'altra volta
quando Bartolo andrà fuori
la consegna ai servitori
a suo modo far saprà.
Eh! non servono le smorfie,
faccia pur la gatta morta.
Cospetton! per quella porta,
nemmen l'aria entrar potrà,
e Rosina innocentina,
sconsolata, disperata,
eh! non servono le smorfie,
faccia pur la gatta morta.
Cospetton! per quella porta
nemmen l'aria entrar potrà.

I advise you, my dear child,
to invent a little better.
Better! Better! Better! Better!
Sweets for Marcellina!
A design for your embroidery!
And the scalding of your finger!
It takes more than that, my girl,
to deceive me successfully.
More! More! More! More!
Why is that sheet of paper missing?
I mean to find out what's going on.
It's no use pulling faces.
Stop, don't touch me.
No, my dear girl, give up all hope
that I'll let myself be fooled.
For a doctor of my standing
these excuses, signorina,
I advise you my dear child,
to invent a little better.
Come, dear child, confess it all.
I am prepared to pardon you.
You don't answer? You are stubborn?
Then I know well what I'll do.
Signorina, another time
when Bartolo must leave the house,
he'll give orders to the servants
who will see you stay inside.
Now your pouting will not help you
nor your injured innocence.
I here assure you, through that door
the very air itself won't enter.
And little innocent Rosina,
disconsolate and in despair,
now your pouting will not help you,
nor your injured innocence.
I here assure you, through that door
the very air itself won't enter,

E Rosina innocentina,
sconsolata, disperata,
in sua camera serrata,
fin ch'io voglio star dovrà.
Sì, sì, sì, sì, ecc.
Un dottor della mia sorte
non si lascia infinocchiar,
e Rosina innocentina, ecc.

and little innocent Rosina,
disconsolate and in despair,
in her chamber shall be locked
so long as I see fit.
Yes, yes, yes, yes, etc.
For a doctor of my standing
does not let himself be fooled.
And little innocent Rosina, etc.

(They exit. Berta enters.)

BERTA
Finora in questa camera
mi parve di sentir un mormorio...
Sarà stato il tutor colla pupilla...
 non ha un'ora di ben.
Queste ragazze non la voglion capir...

BERTA
From within this room
I thought I heard a noise...
Probably the guardian with his ward...
He never has an hour's peace.
These girls don't want to understand...

(She hears a knock and the voice of the Count outside.)

Battono!

Knocking!

CONTE
Aprite.

COUNT
Open.

BERTA

BERTA

(going to open the street door)

Vengo...Eccì...ancora dura:
quel tabacco m'ha posto in sepoltura!

I am coming...A-tishoo..., it keeps on and
on. That snuff has done for me!

(She opens the door. The Count enters disguised as a soldier. He pretends to be drunk. Berta goes out and Bartolo enters.)

CONTE
Ehi, di casa, buona gente...

COUNT
Hey, good people...

niun risponde! Ehi...

BARTOLO
Chi è costui? Che brutta faccia!
È ubbriaco! Chi sarà?

CONTE
Ehi, di casa, maledetti! Ehi...

BARTOLO
Cosa vuol, signor soldato?

CONTE
Ah, sì!
Bene obbligato.

BARTOLO
(Qui costui che mai vorrà?)

CONTE
Siete voi...aspetta un poco...
Siete voi...dottor Balordo?

BARTOLO
Che Balordo? Che Balordo?

CONTE
Ah, ah, Bertoldo?

BARTOLO
Che Bertoldo? Eh, andate al diavolo!
Dottor Bartolo, Dottor Bartolo.

CONTE
Ah, bravissimo;
Dottor Barbaro; bravissimo,
Dottor Barbaro.

Is no one at home! Hey...

BARTOLO
Who can that be? What an ugly face!
And drunk, too! Who is it?

COUNT
Curses, is nobody home! Hey...

BARTOLO
What do you want, signor Soldier?

COUNT
Oh, yes!
Very much obliged.

BARTOLO
(What on earth is he doing here?)

COUNT
You are...wait a minute...
You are... Doctor Balordo?

BARTOLO
What Balordo? What Balordo?

COUNT
Ah, ah, Bertoldo.

BARTOLO
What Bertoldo? Oh, go to the devil!
Doctor Bartolo, Doctor Bartolo.

COUNT
Ah, bravissimo,
Doctor Barbaro, bravissimo,
Doctor Barbaro.

BARTOLO
Un corno!

CONTE
Va benissimo,
già v'è poca differenza.

BARTOLO *(trascinandosi, infuriato)*
(Io già perdo la pazienza.
Qui prudenza ci vorrà.)

CONTE *(in cerca di Rosina)*
(Non si vede! Che impazienza!
Quanto tarda! Dove sta?)
Dunque voi siete dottore?

BARTOLO
Son dottore, sì, signore.

CONTE
Va, benissimo! Un abbraccio,
qua, collega.

BARTOLO
Indietro!

CONTE
Qua. Sono anch'io
dottor per cento...
Maniscalco al reggimento.
Dell'alloggio sul biglietto
osservate, eccolo qua.
(Ah, venisse, il caro oggetto
della mia felicità!)

BARTOLO
(Dalla rabbia, dal dispetto

BARTOLO
You blockhead!

COUNT
Well and good,
the difference, after all, is trifling.

BARTOLO *(shuffling, in a fury)*
(I am already out of patience.
Prudence is necessary here.)

COUNT *(searching for Rosina)*
(She does not appear! How impatient I
feel! How long she delays! Where can she
be?) Then you are a doctor?

BARTOLO
Yes, sir, I am a doctor.

COUNT
Ah, very fine! Let me embrace
a colleague here.

BARTOLO
Keep off!

COUNT
Come. I also am
a qualified doctor,
I am the vet of the regiment.
My billet for lodgings,
look, here it is.
(Oh, come, dearest object
of my happiness!)

BARTOLO
(With rage, with vexation

io già crepo in verità.
Ah, ch'io fo, se mi ci metto,
qualche gran bestialità.)

(Rosina enters from her room.)

CONTE
Vieni, vieni, il tuo diletto,
pien d'amor t'attende già.

BARTOLO
Ah, ch'io fo, se mi ci metto,
qualche gran bestialità!

ROSINA
(Un soldato, il tutore,
cosa mai faranno qua?)

(The Count has seen Rosina and approaches her.)

CONTE
(È Rosina! Or son contento.)

ROSINA
(Ei mi guarda...s'avvicina.)

CONTE
(Son Lindoro!)

ROSINA
(Oh, ciel! Che sento! Ah, giudizio,
ah, giudizio, per pietà!)

BARTOLO *(vedendo Rosina)*
Signorina, che cercate?
Presto, presto, andate via!

in truth I shall burst.
If I don't watch out,
I'll do something rash.)

COUNT
Hasten, hasten, your adorer,
full of love, awaits you here.

BARTOLO
If I don't watch out,
I'll do something rash.

ROSINA
(A soldier, my guardian,
what am I to do now?)

COUNT
(It is Rosina! Now I am happy.)

ROSINA
(He looks at me...he is coming near.)

COUNT
(I am Lindoro!)

ROSINA
(Heavens! What do I hear!
Prudence, for mercy's sake!)

BARTOLO *(seeing Rosina)*
Signorina, what are you looking for?
Quickly, quickly, leave the room!

ROSINA
Vado, vado, non gridate.

BARTOLO
Presto, presto, via di qua.

CONTE
Ehi, ragazza, vengo anch'io.

BARTOLO
Dove, dove, signor mio?

CONTE
In caserma.

BARTOLO
In caserma?

CONTE
Oh, questa è bella!

BARTOLO
In caserma?
Bagatella!

CONTE
Cara...

ROSINA
Aiuto...

BARTOLO
Olà, cospetto!

CONTE
Dunque vado...

ROSINA
I'm going, I'm going, don't shout.

BARTOLO
Quickly, quickly, away from here.

COUNT
And, my girl, I am going too.

BARTOLO
Where, where, sir?

COUNT
To the barracks.

BARTOLO
To the barracks?

COUNT
Oh, this is great!

BARTOLO
To the barracks?
A good joke!

COUNT
Dearest...

ROSINA
Help me...

BARTOLO
Oh, damnation!

COUNT
Then I go...

(The Count starts toward the inner room. Bartolo seizes him.)

BARTOLO
Oh, no signore,
qui d'alloggio non può star.

CONTE
Come? Come?

BARTOLO
Eh, non v'è replica...
Ho il brevetto d'esenzione.

CONTE
Il brevetto?

BARTOLO *(andando allo scrittoio)*
Mio padrone, un momento
e il mostrerò.

CONTE *(piano a Rosina)*
Ah, se qui restar non posso,
deh, prendete...

(He motions to her to take a note.)

ROSINA
(Ohimè! Ci guarda!)

BARTOLO
(Ah, trovarlo ancor non posso.)

ROSINA
(Prudenza!)

BARTOLO
(Ma, sì, sì, lo troverò.)

BARTOLO
Oh, no, sir,
you can have no lodging here.

COUNT
What? What?

BARTOLO
No sense arguing...
I am exempt from lodging troops.

COUNT
Exempt?

BARTOLO *(going to his desk)*
Good sir, just a moment
and I shall show you.

COUNT *(aside to Rosina)*
Since I may not be able to remain here,
take this...

ROSINA
(Be careful! He is watching us!)

BARTOLO
(Oh, I can no longer find it.)

ROSINA
(We must be careful!)

BARTOLO
(But, yes, yes, I must find it.)

ROSINA E CONTE
(Cento smanie io sento addosso,
ah, più reggere non so.)

BARTOLO
Ah, ecco qua.

(He comes forward with a document in his hand and reads.)

"Con la presente il Dottor Bartolo,
eccetera, esentiamo..."

CONTE *(con un rovescio di mano manda in aria
la pergamena)*
Eh, andate al diavolo!
Non mi state più a seccar.

BARTOLO
Cosa fa, signor mio caro?

CONTE *(andando verso Rosina)*
Zitto là, dottor somaro;
il mio alloggio è qui fissato,
e in alloggio qui vo' star.

BARTOLO
Vuol restar?

CONTE
Restar, sicuro.

BARTOLO

(thrashing the Count with his walking stick)

Oh, son stufo, mio padrone,
presto fuori, o un buon bastone

ROSINA AND COUNT
(A hundred emotions burn within me,
I can no longer control myself.)

BARTOLO
Ah, here it is.

"By this let it be known
that Doctor Bartolo etc. is exempted..."

COUNT *(with a sweep of his hand, flings the
paper into the air)*
Oh, go to the devil!
Don't bother me any more.

BARTOLO
My dear sir, what are you doing?

COUNT *(crossing right to Rosina)*
Silence now, donkey of a doctor;
my lodging is fixed here,
and here I will remain.

BARTOLO
Will remain?

COUNT
Certainly, will remain.

BARTOLO

I am fed up, my master,
out and quickly, or a good stick

lo farà di qua sloggiar!

CONTE
Dunque, lei vuol battaglia?
Ben! Battaglia le vo' dar.

(drawing his sword)

Bella cosa è una battaglia!
Ve la voglio qui mostrar.

(He knocks the stick out of Bartolo's hand.)

Osservate! Questo è il fosso...
L'inimico voi sarete...
Attenzion, e gli amici...

(aside to Rosina)

(Giù il fazzoletto.)

(He lets a letter fall and Rosina drops her handkerchief to cover it.)

E gli amici, stan di qua, attenzion.

BARTOLO

(who has noticed the manoeuvre)

Ferma, ferma...

CONTE
Che cos'è? Ah!

BARTOLO
Vo' vedere.

will dislodge you from here!

COUNT
Then you wish to battle?
Good! A battle I will give you.

A battle is a fine thing!
Let me show you how it's done.

Observe! This is the trench...
You are the enemy...
Attention, and my friends...

(Drop your handkerchief.)

And friends standing here. Attention!

BARTOLO

Stop, stop...

COUNT
What is it? Ah!

BARTOLO
Let me see it.

(As Bartolo bends to pick up the letter, the Count puts his sword through it.)

CONTE
Sì, se fosse una ricetta!...
Ma un biglietto...È mio dovere...
Mi dovete perdonar.

COUNT
Yes, if it were a prescription!...
But a note...it is my duty...
If you will pardon me.

(He gives the note to Rosina who quickly exchanges it for a laundry list.)

ROSINA
Grazie, grazie, grazie.

ROSINA
Thank you. Thank you.

BARTOLO
Grazie, grazie, grazie un corno!
Qua quel foglio,
impertinente! A chi dico? Presto qua!

BARTOLO
Thank you, thank you, thank you nothing!
Give me the paper,
impertinent one! Quickly, I say!

CONTE
Vuol battaglia? Attenzion...
Ih! Ah!

COUNT
You wish to battle? On guard...
Ih! Ah!

ROSINA
Ma quel foglio che chiedete
per azzardo m'è cascato.
È la lista del bucato.

ROSINA
But this paper which you ask for
fell to the floor by chance.
It is only the laundry list.

BARTOLO
Ah, fraschetta, presto qua!
Ah, che vedo!

BARTOLO
Oh, you flirt, come quickly here!
What do I see!

(Rosina gives the laundry list to Bartolo; she and the Count cross left. Berta looks through the spy hole of the street door.)

BERTA
Il barbiere...

BERTA
The barber...

BARTOLO
Ho preso abbaglio! È la lista!

BERTA
Quanta gente!

BARTOLO
Son di stucco!

CONTE
Bravo, bravo il mammalucco!

BARTOLO
Ah, son proprio un mammalucco,
oh, che gran bestialità!

(Basilio enters, singing from a sheet of music.)

BASILIO
Sol do re mi fa re sol mi
la fa si sol do,
ma che imbroglio è questo qua.

ROSINA E CONTE
Bravo, bravo il mammalucco
che nel sacco entrato è già.

BERTA
Non capisco, son di stucco,
qualche imbroglio qui ci sta.

ROSINA *(alla fontana, che piange)*
Ecco qua! Sempre un'istoria,
sempre oppressa e maltrattata!
Ah, che vita disperata!
Non la so più sopportar.

BARTOLO
I was mistaken! It is the laundry list!

BERTA
So many people!

BARTOLO
I am petrified!

COUNT
Bravo, bravo, the old fool!

BARTOLO
Yes, I really am an imbecile,
oh, what a big mistake!

BASILIO
Sol do re mi fa re sol mi
la fa si sol do,
but what confusion this is here.

ROSINA AND COUNT
Bravo, bravo, the old fool;
in the trap at last he is caught.

BERTA
I am petrified, bewildered,
what confusion this is here.

ROSINA *(at the fountain, weeping)*
Once again! The same old story,
I am always oppressed and mistreated!
What a wretched life I live!
I can't stand it any more.

BARTOLO
Ah, Rosina poverina...

CONTE

(chases Bartolo away. The others try to restrain him.)

Tu vien qua, cosa le hai fatto?

BARTOLO
Ah, fermate...niente affatto...

CONTE
Ah, canaglia, traditore...

ROSINA, BERTA, BARTOLO E BASILIO
Via, fermatevi, signore.

CONTE
Io ti voglio subissar.

ROSINA E BERTA
Gente, aiuto...ma chetatevi...
Gente, aiuto...per pietà!

BARTOLO E BASILIO
Gente, aiuto...soccorretemi...
Gente, aiuto...per pietà!

CONTE
Lasciatemi, lasciatemi!

(Figaro enters with a basin under his arm.)

FIGARO
Alto là!
Che cosa accadde, signori miei,

BARTOLO
Ah, poor little Rosina.

COUNT

Come here, what have you done to her?

BARTOLO
Stop...nothing at all...

COUNT
You cur, you traitor...

ROSINA, BERTA, BARTOLO AND BASILIO
Hands off, away, sir.

COUNT
I'd like to knock you down.

ROSINA AND BERTA
Good people, help...but calm yourself...
Good people, help...for mercy's sake!

BARTOLO AND BASILIO
Good people, help...help me!
Good people, help...for mercy's sake!

COUNT
Unhand me, unhand me!

FIGARO
Stop!
What is happening,

che chiasso è questo? Eterni dei!
Già sulla strada a questo strepito...
S'è radunata mezza città.

(softly to the Count)

Signor, giudizio, per carità.

BARTOLO *(additando il Conte)*
Quest'è un birbante...

CONTE *(additando Bartolo)*
Quest'è un briccone.

BARTOLO
Ah, disgraziato!

CONTE
Ah, maledetto!

FIGARO
Signor soldato, porti rispetto,
o questo fusto, corpo del diavolo,
or la creanza le insegnerà.
(Signor, giudizio, per carità.)

CONTE
Brutto scimmiotto...

BARTOLO
Birbo malnato...

ROSINA, BERTA, FIGARO E BASILIO
Zitto, dottore...

BARTOLO
Voglio gridare...

what clamour is this? Great gods!
This uproar into the streets
has drawn half the city.

For Heaven's sake, be careful, sir.

BARTOLO *(pointing to the Count)*
This is the rascal.

COUNT *(pointing to Bartolo)*
This is the scoundrel!

BARTOLO
Oh, what a villain!

COUNT
Oh, what a cursed fellow!

FIGARO
Signor Soldier, have respect,
or this basin soon shall teach you
of your manners to beware.
(For Heaven's sake, be careful, sir.)

COUNT
Ugly baboon...

BARTOLO
Low-born scoundrel...

ROSINA, BERTA, FIGARO AND BASILIO
Be quiet, doctor...

BARTOLO
I'll shout it loud...

ROSINA, BERTA, FIGARO E BASILIO
Fermo, signore...

CONTE
Voglio ammazzare...

ROSINA, BERTA, FIGARO E BASILIO
Fate silenzio, per carità!

CONTE
No, voglio ucciderlo,
non v'è pietà.

ROSINA, BERTA, FIGARO E BASILIO
Fate silenzio, per carità!

(loud knocking on the door)

ROSINA, BERTA E FIGARO
Zitti, ché bussano...

TUTTI
Che mai sarà?

BARTOLO *(guardando in strada)*
Chi è?

CORO *(da fuori)*
La forza, la forza, aprite qua!

TUTTI
La forza! oh, diavolo!

FIGARO E BASILIO
L'avete fatta!

ROSINA, BERTA, FIGARO AND BASILIO
Hold, sir...

COUNT
I am going to murder...

ROSINA, BERTA, FIGARO AND BASILIO
Be silent, for pity's sake!

COUNT
I'm going to kill him
without mercy.

ROSINA, BERTA, FIGARO AND BASILIO
Be silent, for pity's sake!

ROSINA, BERTA AND FIGARO
Silence, they are knocking.

ALL
Who can it be?

BARTOLO *(looking out into the street)*
Who's there?

CHORUS *(from without)*
Open the door in the name of the law!

ALL
The police! Oh, the devil!

FIGARO AND BASILIO
Now you have done it!

CONTE E BARTOLO
Niente paura! Venga pur qua.

TUTTI
Quest'avventura, ah!
come diavolo mai finirà!

(An officer, soldiers and townspeople burst into the courtyard.)

CORO
Fermi tutti. Nessun si mova.
Miei signori, che si fa?
Questo chiasso donde è nato?
La cagione presto qua.

BARTOLO
Questa bestia di soldato,
mio signor, m'ha maltrattato,
sì, signor, sì, signor.

FIGARO
Io qua venni, mio signore,
questo chiasso ad acquetar.
Sì, signor, sì, signor.

BASILIO E BERTA
Fa un inferno di rumore,
parla sempre d'ammazzar,
sì, signor, sì, signor.

CONTE
In alloggio quel briccone
non mi volle qui accettar.
Sì, signor, sì, signor.

ROSINA
Perdonate, poverino,

COUNT AND BARTOLO
Have no fear! Let them come in.

ALL
I wonder how on earth
this adventure will end!

CHORUS
Stay where you are. Let no one move.
Good sirs, what's going on?
What is the cause of this disturbance?
Quickly give an explanation.

BARTOLO
This dog of a soldier,
good sir, has mistreated me,
yes, sir, yes, sir.

FIGARO
I only came, good sir,
to calm this disturbance.
Yes, sir, yes, sir.

BASILIO AND BERTA
He is making an infernal noise,
he is threatening to kill us,
yes, sir, yes, sir.

COUNT
As a lodger, this villain
is not willing to accept me.
Yes, sir, yes, sir.

ROSINA
Pardon him, poor fellow,

tutto effetto fu del vino.
Sì, signor, sì, signor.

UFFICIALE
Ho inteso, ho inteso.

(to the Count)

Galantuom, siete in arresto.
Fuori presto, via di qua.

CONTE
In arresto? Io? fermi, olà!

he is affected by wine.
Yes, sir, yes, sir.

OFFICER
I heard you, I heard you.

My good man, you are under arrest.
Quickly come away from here.

COUNT
Arrested? I? Stop now!

(The Count presents a document to the officer who, after reading it, salutes smartly; the soldiers present arms. All remain astonished.)

ROSINA
Fredda ed immobile
come una statua,
fiato non restami
da respirar.

ROSINA
Cold and motionless
like a statue,
I have hardly
breath to breathe!

**disc no. 2
tracks 4 & 5**

Fredda ed immobile...Ma signor...Ma un dottore Everything you have heard so far prepares you for one of the most exuberant and delicious events in the entire operatic literature—a bustling Rossini ensemble that brings down the first act curtain. There is a deceptively calm beginning **(Track 4)**, in which the characters sing of how they are so stupefied by the turn of events they can barely breathe. A gravely beautiful turn of phrase in the orchestra **(03:07)** is dashed with a sudden realization by the characters that they must do something, anything. And they do **(Track 5)**, madly going in all directions until the chaos is too much. To a person, they protest their confusion **(00:25)**, which only gets worse **(01:02)**. It grows into a whirling frenzy **(01:28)**, receding a bit, only to start up again **(02:17)**. The frenzy returns inevitably **(03:17)**, sounding even crazier, as the first act careens to a madcap finish with Rosina's sparkling high notes merrily crowning the ensemble.

CONTE
Freddo ed immobile
come una statua,
fiato non restagli
da respirar!

BARTOLO
Freddo ed immobile
come una statua,
fiato non restami
da respirar!

FIGARO
Guarda Don Bartolo,
sembra una statua!
Ah, ah, dal ridere
sto per crepar!

BASILIO
Freddo ed immobile,
fiato non restami
da respirar!

BERTA
Fiato non restami
da respirar!

BARTOLO
Ma signor...ma un dottor...
ma se lei...ma vorrei...
ma se noi...ma se poi...
ma sentite, ascoltate...

CORO
Zitto, tu! Oh, non più!
Non parlar, non gridar.
Zitti voi! Pensiam noi.

COUNT
Cold and motionless
like a statue,
she has hardly
breath to breathe!

BARTOLO
Cold and motionless
like a statue,
I have hardly
breath to breathe!

FIGARO
Look at Don Bartolo,
he stands like a statue!
Oh, I am ready
to burst with laughter!

BASILIO
Cold and motionless,
I have hardly
breath to breathe!

BERTA
I have hardly
breath to breathe!

BARTOLO
But sir...for a doctor...
But if you...but I would like...
but if we... but if then...
but listen, but hear...

CHORUS
Silence all! That's enough!
Do not speak, do not shout.
Silence! We'll take care of it.

Zitto tu! Non parlar.
Vada ognun pei fatti suoi.
Si finisca d'altercar!

ROSINA E BASILIO
Ma se noi...ma se poi...
ma se poi...ma se noi...
Zitto su! Zitto giù!
Zitto qua! Zitto là!

BERTA, CONTE E FIGARO
Zitto su! Zitto giù!
Zitto qua! Zitto là!

TUTTI
Mi par d'esser con la testa
in un'orrida fucina,
dove cresce e mai non resta
dell'incudini sonore
l'importuno strepitar.
Alternando questo e quello,
pesantissimo martello,
fa con barbara armonia
mure e volte rimbombar.
E il cervello poverello,
già stordito, sbalordito,
non ragiona, si confonde,
si riduce ad impazzar.

Silence you! Do not speak.
Everybody go about their business.
An end to the quarrelling!

ROSINA AND BASILIO
But if we...but if then...
but if then...but if we...
Silence here! Silence there!
Silence, silence everywhere!

BERTA, COUNT AND FIGARO
Silence here! Silence there!
Silence, silence everywhere!

ALL
My head seems to be
in a fiery smithy:
the sound of the anvils
ceaseless and growing
deafens the ear.
Up and down, high and low,
striking heavily, the hammer
makes the very walls resound
with a barbarous harmony.
Thus our poor, bewildered brain,
stunned, confounded,
in confusion, without reason,
is reduced to insanity.

Act 2

THE MUSIC ROOM IN DR BARTOLO'S HOUSE

BARTOLO *(solo)*
Ma vedi il mio destino!
Quel soldato,
per quanto abbia cercato,
niun lo conosce
in tutto il reggimento.
Io dubito...eh, cospetto...
Che dubitar? Scommetto
che dal Conte Almaviva
è stato qui spedito quel signore
ad esplorar della Rosina il core.
(Pesta il piede furiosamente.)
Nemmeno in casa propria
sicuri si può star! Ma io...
(Si sente bussare alla porta principale.)
Chi batte? Ehi, chi è di là!
Battono, non sentite?
In casa io son,
non v'è timore, aprite.

BARTOLO *(alone)*
Look at my ill-fortune!
That soldier,
as far as I can learn,
is known by nobody
in the whole regiment.
I doubt...oh, damnation...
Did I say doubt? I would wager
that the Count Almaviva
has sent this fellow here
to sound out Rosina's heart.
(Angrily he stamps his foot.)
Not even in one's own house
can one be safe! But I...
(Knocks are heard at the main door.)
Who is knocking? Eh, who is there!
They are knocking, don't you hear?
I am home,
have no fear, open.

(The Count enters disguised as a music master.)

CONTE
Pace e gioia sia con voi.

COUNT
Peace and happiness be with you.

BARTOLO
Mille grazie, non s'incomodi.

BARTOLO
A thousand thanks, come right in.

CONTE
Gioia e pace per mill'anni.

COUNT
Happiness and peace for a thousand years.

BARTOLO
Obbligato in verità.
(Questo volto non m'è ignoto.
Non ravviso, non ricordo,
ma quel volto, ma quel volto...
Non capisco, chi sarà?)

CONTE
(Ah, se un colpo è andato a vuoto
a gabbar questo balordo
un novel travestimento
più propizio a me sarà.)
Gioia e pace sia con voi.

BARTOLO
Ho capito! (Oh, ciel! Che noia!)

CONTE
Gioia e pace, ben di core.

BARTOLO
Basta, basta, per pietà.

CONTE
Gioia...

BARTOLO
Gioia...

CONTE
Pace...

BARTOLO
Pace...Ho capito! (Oh ciel! Che noia!)

CONTE
Ben di core, pace e gioia.

BARTOLO
In truth I am obliged to you.
(That face is not unknown to me.
I don't recall, I don't remember,
but that face, that face...
I do not know, who can it be?)

COUNT
(Ah, if before I failed
to deceive this simpleton,
my new disguise should prove
more successful.)
Peace and happiness be with you.

BARTOLO
I heard you! (Heavens, what a bore!)

COUNT
Happiness and peace, from my heart.

BARTOLO
Enough, enough, for pity's sake.

COUNT
Happiness...

BARTOLO
Happiness...

COUNT
Peace...

BARTOLO
Peace...I heard you! (What a bore!)

COUNT
From my heart, peace and happiness.

BARTOLO
Pace a gioia. Basta, basta, per pietà!
(Ma che perfido destino!
Ma che barbara giornata!
Tutti quanti a me davanti!
Che crudel fatalità!)

CONTE
(Il vecchion non mi conosce,
oh, mia sorte fortunata!
Ah, mio ben! Fra pochi istanti
parlerem con libertà!)

BARTOLO

(hastening to prevent the Count from starting all over again)

Insomma, mio signore, chi è lei?
Si può sapere?

CONTE
Don Alonso, professore di musica
ed allievo di Don Basilio.

BARTOLO
Ebbene?

CONTE
Don Basilio sta male, il poverino,
ed in sua vece...

BARTOLO
Sta mal? Corro a vederlo.

CONTE
Piano, piano. Non è mal così grave.

BARTOLO
Peace and happiness. Enough, for pity's
sake!
(What a wretched fate is mine!
What a terrible day this is!
Everyone against me!
What a cruel destiny!)

COUNT
(The old fellow knows me not.
How fortunate for me!
Ah, my love! In a few moments
we shall be able to speak freely!)

BARTOLO

In a word, sir, who are you?
May one know?

COUNT
Don Alonso, teacher of music
and pupil of Don Basilio.

BARTOLO
Well?

COUNT
Don Basilio, poor man, is taken ill,
and in his stead...

BARTOLO
Taken ill? I'll go and see him at once.

COUNT
Take it easy. His illness is not that serious.

BARTOLO
(Di costui non mi fido.)
Andiamo, andiamo.

CONTE
Ma signore...

BARTOLO
Cosa c'è?

CONTE
Voleva dirvi...

BARTOLO
Parlate forte.

CONTE (sottovoce)
Ma...

BARTOLO
Forte, vi dico.

CONTE
Ebben, come volete,
ma chi sia Don Alonso apprenderete.

(raising his voice)

Vo' dal Conte Almaviva...

BARTOLO
Piano, piano, dite, dite.
V'ascolto.

CONTE
Il Conte...

BARTOLO
(I don't trust this fellow.)
Come, let us go.

COUNT
But sir...

BARTOLO
Well, what?

COUNT
I wished to say...

BARTOLO
Speak up.

COUNT (sottovoce)
But...

BARTOLO
Speak up, I tell you.

COUNT
Well, as you wish.
Then you shall learn who Don Alonso is.

I come from Count Almaviva...

BARTOLO
Softly, softly, speak, speak.
I am listening.

COUNT
The Count...

BARTOLO
Pian, per carità!

CONTE
Stamane, nella stessa locanda
era meco d'alloggio,
ed in mie mani, per caso
(dando a Bartolo una lettera di Rosina)
capitò questo biglietto
della vostra pupilla
a lui diretto.

BARTOLO
Che vedo? È sua scrittura!

CONTE
Don Basilio nulla sa di quel foglio,
ed io, per lui venendo
a dar lezione alla ragazza,
voleva farmene un merito con voi...
perché con quel biglietto...si potrebbe...

BARTOLO
Che cosa?

CONTE
Vi dirò...s'io potessi
 parlare alla ragazza, io creder...
verbigrazia...le farei
che me lo die' del Conte un'altra amante,
prova significante
che il Conte di Rosina si fa gioco,
e perciò...

BARTOLO
Piano un poco...Una calunnia!
Oh, bravo, degno e vero scolar

BARTOLO
Softly, for goodness' sake!

COUNT
This morning I met him in the same inn
where I was lodging,
and into my hand, by chance,
(giving Bartolo one of Rosina's letters)
fell this note,
addressed by your ward
to him.

BARTOLO
What do I see! It is her writing!

COUNT
Don Basilio knows nothing of this paper,
and I, coming instead of him
to give lessons to the young lady,
wished to acquire merit in your eyes
because with this note...one could...

BARTOLO
Could what?

COUNT
I shall tell you...If I could only
speak with the girl, I could...
with your permission...make her believe
that it was given to me by a mistress
of the Count, clear proof
that the Count is playing with her affection, and therefore...

BARTOLO
Softly...A calumny!
Oh, you are indeed a worthy pupil

di Don Basilio!
Io saprò, come merita, ricompensar
sì bel suggerimento. Vo' a chiamar
la ragazza. Poiché tanto per me
v'interessate, mi raccomando a voi.

CONTE
Non dubitate.

(Bartolo goes to fetch Rosina.)

L'affare del biglietto
dalla bocca m'è uscito non volendo.
Ma come far? Senza un tal ripiego,
mi toccava andar via come un baggiano.
Il mio disegno
a lei ora paleserò;
s'ella acconsente,
io son felice appieno.
Eccola. Ah, il cor sento
balzarmi in seno!

(Bartolo returns leading Rosina by the hand.)

BARTOLO
Venite, signorina.
Don Alonso, che qui vedete,
or vi darà lezione.

ROSINA *(vedendo il Conte)*
Ah!

BARTOLO
Cos'è stato?

ROSINA
È un granchio al piede.

of Don Basilio!
I shall know how to reward you
as you deserve for this happy suggestion.
I'll call the girl. Since you show
so much interest, I trust myself to you.

COUNT
Do not worry.

This affair of the note
was a slip of the tongue.
But what was I to do? Without some trick,
I would have had to leave like a fool.
I must now acquaint her
with my plan;
if she consents,
I shall be a happy man.
Here she is. Oh, how my heart
is beating in my breast!

BARTOLO
Come, Signorina.
Don Alonso, whom you see,
will give you your lesson.

ROSINA *(recognizing the Count)*
Ah!

BARTOLO
What's the matter?

ROSINA
Oh...a cramp in my foot.

CONTE (*conducendola al clavicembalo*)
Oh, nulla! Sedete a me vicin,
bella fanciulla. Se non vi spiace
un poco di lezione
di Don Basilio invece vi darò.

ROSINA
Oh, con mio gran piacere la prenderò.

CONTE
Che volete cantar?

ROSINA
Io canto, se le aggrada,
il rondò dell'Inutil precauzione.

BARTOLO
Eh, sempre, sempre in bocca
L'Inutil precauzione!

ROSINA
Io ve l'ho detto:
è il titolo dell'opera novella.

BARTOLO
Orbene, intesi; andiamo.

ROSINA
Eccolo qua.

CONTE
Da brava, incominciamo.

(He sits down at the harpsichord and accompanies Rosina.)

ROSINA
Contro un cor che accende amore

COUNT (*taking her to the harpsichord*)
Oh, it's nothing! Sit by my side,
fair young lady. If you don't mind,
in place of Don Basilio,
I shall give you a short lesson.

ROSINA
Oh, with the greatest of pleasure.

COUNT
What would you like to sing?

ROSINA
I shall sing, if you please,
the rondo from The Futile Precaution.

BARTOLO
Oh, you're always prating
about The Futile Precaution.

ROSINA
I told you:
it's the title of the new opera.

BARTOLO
Very well, Iunderstand; come now.

ROSINA
Here it is.

COUNT
Good, let's begin.

ROSINA
Against a heart inflamed with love,

di verace invitto ardore,
s'arma invan poter tiranno
di rigor, di crudeltà.
D'ogni assalto vincitore,
sempre amore trionferà.

burning with unquenchable fire,
a ruthless tyrant, cruelly armed,
wages war, but all in vain.
From every attack a victor,
Love will always triumph.

(Bartolo has gone to sleep in the armchair.)

Ah, Lindoro, mio tesoro.
Se sapessi, se vedessi,
questo cane di tutore,
ah, che rabbia che mi fa!
Caro, a te mi raccomando,
tu mi salva, per pietà!

Ah, Lindoro, my dearest treasure!
If you could know, if you could see
this dog of a guardian,
oh, I rage to think of him!
Dearest, in you I put my trust,
please, come save me, for pity's sake!

CONTE
Non temer, ti rassicura,
sorte amica a noi sarà.

COUNT
Fear not, be reassured,
fate will be our friend.

ROSINA
Dunque spero?

ROSINA
Then I may hope?

CONTE
A me t'affida.

COUNT
Trust in me.

ROSINA
E il mio cor?

ROSINA
And my heart?

CONTE
Giubilerà!

COUNT
It will rejoice!

ROSINA
Cara immagine ridente,
dolce idea d'un lieto amor,
tu m'accendi in petto, il core.
Tu mi porti a delirar!
Caro, a te mi raccomando,

ROSINA
Dear smiling image,
sweet thought of happy love,
you burn in my breast, in my heart.
I am delirious with joy!
Dearest, in you I put my trust,

tu mi salva, per pietà!
tu mi porti a delirar!

CONTE
Bella voce! Bravissima!

ROSINA
Oh! Mille grazie!

BARTOLO

(waking up and crossing to harpsichord)

Certo, bella voce!
Ma quest'aria, cospetto!
è assai noiosa.
La musica a' miei tempi
era altra cosa.
Ah! Quando, per esempio, cantava
Caffariello quell'aria portentosa...
La ra la la la...sentite,
Don Alonso, eccola qua.
"Quando mi sei vicina,
amabile Rosina..."

(Figaro enters and hides behind Bartolo.)

L'aria dicea "Giannina",
ma io dico "Rosina..."
"Quando mi sei vicina,
amabile Rosina,
il cor mi brilla in petto.
Mi balla il minuetto..."

(He dances a courtly step. He notices the presence of Figaro who is imitating him behind his back.)

COUNT
A beautiful voice! Bravissima!

ROSINA
Oh! A thousand thanks!

BARTOLO

Truly, a beautiful voice!
But this aria, damnation!
It is rather tiresome.
Music in my day
was quite another thing.
Ah! When, for instance,
Caffariello sang that wonderful aria...
la ra la la la...Listen,
Don Alonso, here it is.
"When you are near me,
Sweet Rosina..."

The aria says "Giannina",
but I say "Rosina..."
"When you are near me,
sweet Rosina,
my heart glows in my breast,
it dances a minuet..."

Bravo, signor barbiere, ma bravo!

FIGARO
Eh, niente affatto, scusi,
son debolezze...

BARTOLO
Ebben, guidone, che vieni a fare?

FIGARO
Oh, bella! Vengo a farvi la barba!
Oggi vi tocca.

BARTOLO
Oggi non voglio.

FIGARO
Oggi non vuol?
Dimani non potrò io.

BARTOLO
Perché?

FIGARO (consultando il suo diario)
Perché ho da fare.
A tutti gli Uffiziali
del nuovo reggimento
barba e testa,
alla Marchesa Andronica
il biondo parruchin
coi maroné...
Al Contino Bombè
il ciuffo a campanile...
Purgante all'avvocato Bernardone
che ieri s'ammalò d'indigestione.
E poi...e poi...che serve?
Doman non posso.

Bravo, signor Barber, bravo!

FIGARO
Excuse me please,
it was a moment of weakness...

BARTOLO
Well, you rascal, what are you here for?

FIGARO
Here for! Here to shave you.
This is your day.

BARTOLO
I don't wish it today.

FIGARO
Today you don't wish it?
Tomorrow I can't come.

BARTOLO
Why not?

FIGARO (consulting his notebook)
Because I shall be busy.
For all the officers
of the new regiment,
shave and haircut...
For the Marchioness Andronica,
her blond wig
tinted brown...
For the young Count Bombè,
forelock to curl...
A purge for the lawyer Bernardone
who yesterday fell ill with indigestion.
And then...and then...but why continue?
Tomorrow I cannot come.

BARTOLO

Orsù, meno parole.
Oggi non vo' far barba.

FIGARO

No? Cospetto! Guardate che avventori!
Vengo stamane, in casa v'è l'inferno...
Ritorno dopo pranzo...
Oggi non voglio.
Ma che? M'avete preso
per un qualche barbier da contadini?
Chiamate pur un altro.

(pretending to leave)

Io me ne vado.

BARTOLO

(Che serve? A modo suo.
Vedi che fantasia!)

(calling him back and holding out a bunch of keys to him)

Va in camera a pigliar la biancheria.
No, vado io stesso.

(He snatches back the bunch of keys before Figaro can take them.)

FIGARO

(Ah, se mi dava in mano
il mazzo delle chiavi
ero a cavallo.) Dite,

(to Rosina)

non è fra quelle

BARTOLO

Come, less chatter.
Today I do not want to be shaved.

FIGARO

No? Nice kind of customers I have!
I come this morning, and I find a
madhouse...
I return after lunch...
Today I don't want you!
What do you think? Do you take me
for some country barber?
Find yourself another.

I am going.

BARTOLO

(What can one do? That's how he is.
He is really a character!)

Go into the next room and bring the towels.
No, I'll go myself.

FIGARO

Oh, if I had those keys
in my hand
I should be riding high. Tell me,

among the keys, isn't there the one

la chiave che apre quella gelosia?

ROSINA
Sì, certo. È la più nuova.

(Bartolo returns.)

BARTOLO
(Ah, son pur buono
a lasciar quel diavol di barbiere!)
Animo, va tu stesso.

(He gives the keys to Figaro.)

Passato il corridor, sopra l'armadio
il tutto troverai.
Bada, non toccar nulla.

FIGARO
Eh! Non son matto.
(Allegri!) Vado e torno.
(Il colpo è fatto!)

(He goes out.)

BARTOLO *(prendendo da parte il Conte)*
È quel briccon che al Conte
ha portato il biglietto di Rosina...

CONTE
Mi sembra un imbroglion di prima sfera.

BARTOLO
Ehi! A me non me la ficca...

(A great noise is heard without.)

which opens the outside window?

ROSINA
Yes, indeed. It is the newest.

BARTOLO
(Oh, what a fool I was
to leave that devil of a barber here!)
Here, go yourself.

Go down the corridor, and on the shelf
you'll find everything.
Take care, don't touch anything.

FIGARO
Oh! I know what I am doing.
(Brilliant!) I'll be right back.
(The trick has worked!)

BARTOLO *(taking the Count aside)*
That is the rascal who took
Rosina's letter to the Count...

COUNT
He looks like an intriguer of the first order.

BARTOLO
He can't deceive me...

Ah, disgraziato me!

ROSINA
Ah, che rumore!

BARTOLO
Oh, che briccon!
Me lo diceva il core!

(Bartolo goes out.)

CONTE
Quel Figaro è un grand'uomo!

(to Rosina)

Or che siam soli, ditemi, o cara,
il vostro al mio destino
d'unir siete contenta?
Franchezza!

ROSINA
Ah! mio Lindoro, altro
io non bramo...

(Bartolo and Figaro return.)

CONTE
Ebben?

BARTOLO
Tutto m'ha rotto, sei piatti,
otto bicchieri, una terrina.

FIGARO
Vedete che gran cosa!

Oh, misery me!

ROSINA
What a crash!

BARTOLO
Oh, that rascal!
I felt my heart misgive me!

COUNT
That Figaro is a great man!

Now that we are alone, tell me dearest,
are you content to put your destiny
in my hands?
Be frank now!

ROSINA
Ah, Lindoro, it is
my only desire...

COUNT
Well?

BARTOLO
He has broken everything, six plates,
eight glasses, a tureen.

FIGARO
What good luck!

(Secretly he shows the Count the key of the balcony window which he has taken.)

Ad una chiave se io non m'attaccava
per fortuna, per quel maledettissimo corridor
così oscuro, spezzato mi sarei
la testa al muro. Tiene ogni stanza
al buio...e poi...

BARTOLO
Oh, non più...

FIGARO
Dunque andiam.

(to the Count and Rosina)

(Giudizio.)

If I had not held on to a key
I would have broken my head
in that cursed corridor.
He keeps every room
so dark...and then...

BARTOLO
Enough of this...

FIGARO
Then let's get going.

(Be careful.)

(Bartolo prepares to be shaved.)

BARTOLO
A noi.

BARTOLO
Now to business.

(Don Basilio enters.)

disc no. 2/track 14 *Don Basilio!...Cosa veggo* The whole ruse threatens to come crashing down with the arrival of the real Don Basilio. Rossini treats the moment as a rollicking, virtuosic ensemble set-piece; hearing it is like watching an intricate machine with hundreds of parts, all running smoothly. Listen, at any random moment, to the way the musical line captures the emotion or intention of what the character sings. The orchestral accompaniment is deft and simple, keeping the action of the characters in the forefront. Basilio finally announces his departure, and he is bid farewell by everyone (04:26) with a sunny melody that feigns good will, though he can't leave quickly enough for them. The violins play a skittish little figure (06:50) that sets up the action that follows: Figaro shaves Bartolo, while the dis-guised Count and Rosina (supposedly having a music lesson) plot their departure. The transparency of the music adds shivers of excitement to the sly deceptions at work here. But Bartolo overhears (08:59), and explodes in a rage. Rossini spins out another fizzy little melody that sets up the frantic coda to the whole scene (09:20).

ROSINA
(Don Basilio!)

ONTE
(Cosa veggo!)

FIGARO
(Quale intoppo!)

BARTOLO
Come qua?

BASILIO
Servitor, di tutti quanti.

BARTOLO
(Che vuol dir tal novità?)

ROSINA
(Di noi che mai sarà?)

CONTE E FIGARO
(Qui franchezza ci vorrà.)

BARTOLO
Don Basilio, come state?

BASILIO
Come sto?...

FIGARO
Or che s'aspetta?
Questa barba benedetta,
la facciamo sì o no?

ROSINA
Don Basilio!

COUNT
(What do I see!)

FIGARO
(How unfortunate!)

BARTOLO
How come you are here?

BASILIO
At your service, one and all.

BARTOLO
(What is this new turn of affairs?)

ROSINA
(What will happen to us?)

COUNT AND FIGARO
(We must act boldly.)

BARTOLO
Don Basilio, how are you feeling?

BASILIO
How am I feeling?

FIGARO
What are you waiting for?
That blessed beard of yours,
shall I shave it or not?

113

BARTOLO *(a Figaro)*
Ora vengo.

(to Basilio)

E...il curiale?

BASILIO
Il curiale...

CONTE
Io gli ho narrato
che già tutto è combinato.

(to Bartolo)

Non è ver?

BARTOLO
Sì, sì, tutto io so.

BASILIO
Ma, Don Bartolo, spiegatevi...

CONTE

(drawing Bartolo aside to separate him from Basilio)

Ehi, dottore, una parola...
Don Basilio, son da voi.

(to Bartolo)

Ascoltate un poco qua.

(aside to Figaro)

BARTOLO *(to Figaro)*
In a minute.

And...the notary?

BASILIO
The notary...

COUNT
I have already told him
that everything is arranged.

Is it not true?

BARTOLO
Yes, yes I know it all.

BASILIO
But, Don Bartolo, explain to me...

COUNT

Doctor, one word...
Don Basilio, I'll be with you.

Listen to me for a moment.

Fate un po' ch'ei vada via,
ch'ei ci scopra ho gran timore.

ROSINA
(Io mi sento il cor tremar.)

FIGARO
(Non vi state a disperar.)

CONTE *(a Bartolo)*
Della lettera, signore,
ei l'affare ancor non sa.

BASILIO
(Ah, qui certo v'è un pasticcio,
non s'arriva a indovinar.)

CONTE
(Ch'ei ci scopra ho gran timore;
ei l'affare ancor non sa.)

BARTOLO
(Dite bene, mio signore,
or lo mando via di qua.)

CONTE
Colla febbre, Don Basilio,
chi v'insegna colla febbre a passeggiare?

BASILIO
Colla febbre?

CONTE
E che vi pare?
Siete giallo come un morto.

Try and get rid of him,
or I fear he will expose us.

ROSINA
I feel my heart tremble.

FIGARO
Don't be alarmed.

COUNT *(to Bartolo)*
Of the letter, sir,
he as yet knows nothing.

BASILIO
(There is something going on
which I certainly cannot fathom.)

COUNT
I fear he will expose us;
he as yet knows nothing.

BARTOLO
You are right, sir.
I will immediately send him away.

COUNT
With such a fever, Don Basilio,
who told you to go out?

BASILIO
What fever?

COUNT
What do you think?
You are yellow as a corpse.

BASILIO
Sono giallo come un morto?

FIGARO (*tastando il polso di Basilio*)
Bagatella! Cospetton!
Che tremarella!
Questa è febbre scarlattina!

BASILIO
Scarlattina!

CONTE

(*secretly handing Basilio a purse of money*)

Via, prendete medicina.
Non vi state a rovinar.

FIGARO
Presto, presto, andate a letto.

CONTE
Voi paura inver mi fate.

ROSINA
Dice bene, andate a letto...

BARTOLO, ROSINA, CONTE E
FIGARO
Presto, andate a riposar.

BASILIO
(Una borsa!...andate a letto!
Ma che tutti sian d'accordo!)

BASILIO
I am yellow as a corpse?

FIGARO (*feeling Basilio's pulse*)
Good Heaven, my man,
you are all of a tremble!
You must have scarlet fever!

BASILIO
Scarlet fever!

COUNT

Go take some medicine.
Don't stay here and kill yourself.

FIGARO
Quickly, quickly, go to bed.

COUNT
I am really afraid for you.

ROSINA
He is right, go home to bed...

BARTOLO, ROSINA, COUNT AND
FIGARO
Quickly, go and have some rest.

BASILIO
(A purse!...Go to bed!
As long as they are all of one mind!)

BARTOLO, ROSINA, CONTE E FIGARO
Presto a letto, presto a letto...

BASILIO
Eh, non son sordo,
non mi faccio più pregar.

FIGARO
Che color!...

CONTE
Che brutta cera!...

BASILIO
Brutta cera?

CONTE, FIGARO, E BARTOLO
Oh, brutta assai!...

BASILIO
Dunque vado!...

ROSINA, CONTE, FIGARO E BARTOLO
Vada. Vada.

CONTE, ROSINA E FIGARO
Buona sera, mio signore,
presto andate via di qua.

BASILIO
Buona sera, ben di core...
Poi diman si parlerà.

ROSINA E FIGARO
Maledetto seccatore,

BARTOLO, ROSINA, COUNT AND FIGARO
Quickly to bed, quickly to bed...

BASILIO
I am not deaf,
you don't have to beg me.

FIGARO
What a colour!

COUNT
You look terribe!

BASILIO
Terrible?

COUNT, FIGARO AND BARTOLO
Oh, really terrible!

BASILIO
Well, I'll go!

ROSINA, COUNT, FIGARO AND BARTOLO
Go, go.

COUNT, ROSINA AND FIGARO
Well, good-night to you, dear sir,
quickly go away from here.

BASILIO
Well, good-night, with all my heart,
then tomorrow we shall talk.

ROSINA AND FIGARO
Cursed man, you are a nuisance!

buona sera, mio signore,
pace, sonno e sanità,
buona sera, via di qua,
presto, andate via di qua.

CONTE
Buona sera, via di qua,
buona sera, mio signore,
pace, sonno e sanità,
presto andate via di qua.

BARTOLO
Buona sera, mio signore,
pace, sonno e sanità,
presto, andate via di qua.

BASILIO
Buona sera, ben di core,
poi diman si parlerà.
Non gridate, per pietà.

(Basilio goes out.)

FIGARO
Orsù, Signor Don Bartolo.

BARTOLO
Son qua. Son qua.

(Figaro starts to shave Don Bartolo and at the same time tries to conceal the two lovers.)

Stringi. Bravissimo.

CONTE
Rosina, deh, ascoltatemi.

Well, good-night to you, dear sir,
peace and slumber and good health.
Well, good-night, get out of here,
quickly go away from here.

COUNT
Well, good-night, away from here.
Well, good-night to you, dear sir,
peace and slumber and good health.
Quickly go away from here.

BARTOLO
Well, good-night to you, dear sir,
peace and slumber and good health.
Quickly go away from here.

BASILIO
Well, good-night, with all my heart,
then tomorrow we shall talk.
Do not shout, for pity's sake!

FIGARO
Well, signor Don Bartolo.

BARTOLO
I am here. I am here.

Pull it tight. Bravissimo.

COUNT
Rosina, listen to me.

ROSINA
V'ascolto. Eccomi qua.

ROSINA
I am listening. I am here.

(The Count and Rosina sit on the harpsichord stool pretending to study.)

CONTE
A mezzanotte in punto
a prendervi qui siamo.
Or che la chiave abbiamo
non v'è da dubitar.

COUNT
At midnight precisely
we'll come for you here.
And since we have the keys
there is nothing to fear.

FIGARO
Ahi! Ahi!

FIGARO
Ah! Ah!

BARTOLO
Che cosa è stato?

BARTOLO
What's the matter?

FIGARO
Un non so che nell'occhio!...
Guardate!...Non toccate...
Soffiate, per pietà!

FIGARO
Something, I don't know what,
is in my eye!...Look...Don't touch it...
Blow into it, for pity's sake!

ROSINA
A mezzanotte in punto,
anima mia, t'aspetto.
Io già l'istante affretto
che a te mi stringerà.

ROSINA
At midnight precisely,
my love, I shall await you.
May the moments hasten
which draw you to me.

(Bartolo has become suspicious of the music lesson; he creeps over to the harpsichord while the Count is singing.)

CONTE
Ora avvertir vi voglio,
cara, che il vostro foglio,
perché non fosse inutile
il mio travestimento...

COUNT
But now I must tell you,
dearest, that your letter,
in order that I might succeed
in my disguise...

BARTOLO
Il suo travestimento?

BARTOLO
In his disguise?

(The Count and Rosina jump up and retreat around the harpsichord.)

Ah! Bravi, bravissimo!
Signor Alonso, bravo! bravi!
Bricconi! Birbanti!
Ah! voi tutti quanti
avete giurato di farmi crepar.

Ah! Bravi, bravissimi!
Signor Alonso, bravo! Bravi!
Rascals! Scoundrels!
Ah! I can see you have all sworn
to hasten my end.

(He chases all three around the room.)

Su, fuori, furfanti,
vi voglio accoppar!

Out, you villains,
or I shall kill you!

ROSINA, CONTE E FIGARO
La testa vi gira,
ma zitto, dottore,
vi fate burlar.
Tacete, tacete,
non serve gridare.
L'amico delira.
(Intesi già siamo,
non vo' replicar.)
Non serve gridar.

ROSINA, COUNT AND FIGARO
Your head is spinning,
hush, good doctor,
you are making a fool of yourself.
Be quiet, be quiet,
it's senseless to shout.
This man is delirious.
(Now that it's settled
I don't have to repeat.)
It is senseless to shout.

BARTOLO
Bricconi! birbanti!
Su, fuori, furfanti,
vi voglio accoppare.
Avete giurato di farmi crepare.
Di rabbia, di sdegno,
mi sento crepare,
vi voglio accoppar.

BARTOLO
Rascals, scoundrels!
Out, you villains,
or I shall kill you!
You have all sworn to hasten my end.
I'm fairly bursting
with anger and disdain.
I shall kill you!

(Bartolo has won the battle. The Count and Figaro run out of the house, Bartolo follows them, and Rosina escapes to her room. Berta enters.)

BERTA
Che vecchio sospettoso!
Vada pure e ci stia finché crepa!
Sempre gridi e tumulti in questa casa...
Si litiga...si piange...si minaccia...
Sì, non v'è un'ora di pace
con questo vecchio avaro e brontolone.
Oh che casa in confusione!

(She begins to tidy the room.)

Il vecchiotto cerca moglie,
vuol marito la ragazza,
quello freme, questa è pazza,
tutti e due son da legar.
Ma che cosa è quest'amore
che fa tutti delirar?
Egli è un male universale,
una smania, un pizzicore,
un solletico, un tormento,
poverina, anch'io lo sento
né so come finirà.
Oh, vecchietta maledetta!
Son da tutti disprezzata,
e vecchietta disperata
mi convien così crepar.

(Berta goes out. Bartolo enters with Basilio.)

BARTOLO
Dunque voi don Alonso
non conoscete affatto?

BASILIO
Affatto.

BERTA
What a suspicious old man!
Begone and don't come back alive!
Always shouting and clamour in this house...
Arguing...weeping...threatening...
There is not an hour's peace
with this stingy, grumbling old man.
Oh, what a house of confusion!

The old man seeks a wife,
and the maiden wants a husband,
the one is frenzied, the other crazy,
both of them need restraining.
What on earth is all this love
which makes everyone go mad?
It is a universal evil,
it is a mania and an itch,
a thing which tickles and torments you.
Unhappy me, I also feel it
and do not know how to escape.
Oh, accursed old maid!
By all I am despised,
an old maid without a hope,
I shall die in desperation.

BARTOLO
So you don't know
a Don Alonso?

BASILIO
Certainly not.

BARTOLO
Ah, certo. Il Conte lo mandò.
Qualche gran tradimento si prepara.

BASILIO
Io poi dico che quell'amico
era il Conte in persona.

BARTOLO
Il Conte?

BASILIO
Il Conte.
(La borsa parla chiaro.)

BARTOLO
Sia chi si vuole...
Amico, dal notaro
vo' in questo punto andare;
in questa sera stipular
di mie nozze io vo' il contratto.

BASILIO
Il notar? Siete matto?
Piove a torrenti, e poi
questa sera il notaro
è impegnato con Figaro;
il barbiere marita sua nipote.

BARTOLO
Una nipote? Che nipote?
Il barbiere non ha nipoti...
Ah, qui v'è qualche imbroglio.
Questa notte i bricconi
me la vogliono far;
presto, il notaro qua venga

BARTOLO
Ah, of course, the Count must have sent
him. They're hatching some monstrous
plot.

BASILIO
I say that our friend
was the Count in person.

BARTOLO
The Count?

BASILIO
The Count.
(The purse he gave me speaks for itself.)

BARTOLO
I don't care who it was...
My friend, I'm off
to see the notary at once;
I'll have the marriage contract
drawn up tonight.

BASILIO
The notary! Are you mad?
It's pouring with rain. Besides,
tonight the notary
is seeing Figaro;
the barber is fixing up his niece's marriage.

BARTOLO
His niece? What niece?
The barber has no nieces...
Aha, there's dirty work afoot.
Tonight the rogues
mean to trick me;
quick, bring the notary here

sull'istante...
Ecco la chiave del portone:

immediately...
Here's the front door key.

(Bartolo gives Basilio the front door key and pushes him out.)

Andate, presto, per carità.

Hurry, hurry, for Heaven's sake.

BASILIO
Non temete: in due salti io torno qua.

BASILIO
Never fear: I'll be back in two shakes.

(He leaves.)

BARTOLO
Per forza o per amore Rosina
avrà da cedere.
Cospetto! Mi vien un'altra idea.
Questo biglietto che scrisse
la ragazza ad Almaviva potria servir...
Che colpo da maestro!
Don Alonso, il briccone, senza volerlo mi
diè l'armi in
mano.
Ehi! Rosina, Rosina.

BARTOLO
Whether she likes it or not
Rosina will have to yield.
By Jove! I've another idea.
This letter the minx wrote
to Almaviva might serve...
what a masterstroke!
That rascal Don Alonso has given me the
weapon I need willy-
nilly.
Hey! Rosina, Rosina.

(Rosina enters from her room.)

Avanti, avanti,
del vostro amante io vi vo' dar novella.
Povera sciagurata!
In verità collocaste assai bene il vostro
affetto!
Del vostro amor sappiate ch'ei si fa gioco
in sen d'un'altra amante, ecco la prova.

Come here,
I've some news of your lover for you.
Poor, unhappy girl!
You've certainly bestowed your affections
on a fine rascal!
You should know that he's laughing
at your love in the arms of another woman,
here's the proof.

(He shows Rosina her letter, but hangs on to it.)

ROSINA
Oh, cielo, il mio biglietto!

BARTOLO
Don Alonso e il barbiere
congiuran contro voi,
non vi fidate.
Nelle braccia del Conte Almaviva
vi vogliono condurre.

ROSINA
In braccio a un altro!
Che mai sento!
Ah, Lindoro! ah, traditore!
Ah, sì!...vendetta!
E vegga quell'empio chi è Rosina.
Dite, signore, di sposarmi voi bramavate...

BARTOLO
E il voglio.

ROSINA
Ebben, si faccia! Io son contenta!
Ma all'istante.
Udite: a mezzanotte
qui sarà l'indegno con Figaro il barbier;
con lui fuggire per sposarlo io voleva...

BARTOLO
Ah! scellerati! Corro a sbarrar la porta...

ROSINA
Ah! mio signore! Entran per la finestra.
Hanno la chiave.

ROSINA
Oh, heavens, my letter!

BARTOLO
Don Alonso and the barber
are plotting against you,
don't trust them.
They intend to deliver
you into the arms of Count Almaviva.

ROSINA
Into another's arms!
What's that you say?
Ah, Lindoro! You traitor!
Ah, so!...revenge!
This wicked one shall see who Rosina is.
Sir, you always wanted to marry me...

BARTOLO
And I still do.

ROSINA
Well then, you shall! I'm...happy to.
But we must wed at once.
Listen: at midnight
the wretch will be here with Figaro, the
barber. I was going
to elope with him...

BARTOLO
The scoundrels! I'll run and bar the door...

ROSINA
Oh, Sir! They're going to come in through
the window. They've got the key.

BARTOLO
Non mi muovo di qui!
Ma...e se fossero armati?
Figlia mia, poiché ti sei
sì bene illuminata, facciam così.
Chiuditi a chiave in camera,
io vo' a chiamar la forza;
dirò che son due ladri, e come tali,
corpo di Bacco! L'avremo da vedere!
Figlia, chiuditi presto:
io vado via.

BARTOLO
I'll not budge from here!
But...suppose they're armed.
My child, as you are now
so well informed, let us do this.
Lock yourself in your room,
I'm going to call the law;
I shall say that they are two robbers and so,
the deuce! We'll see about that!
My child, lock yourself in:
I'm off.

(Bartolo runs out of the house.)

ROSINA
Quanto, quanto è crudel la sorte mia!

ROSINA
What a bitterly cruel fate is mine!

(Rosina goes to her room.)

(Storm—It is night. The balcony window is opened. Figaro and the Count wrapped in mantles enter. Figaro carries a lantern.)

FIGARO
Alfine eccoci qua.

FIGARO
At last we are here.

CONTE
Figaro, dammi man.
Poter del mondo!
Che tempo indiavolato!

COUNT
Figaro, give me your hand.
Thunder and lightning!
What wicked weather!

FIGARO
Tempo da innamorati!

FIGARO
What a night for lovers!

(The Count stumbles over the harpsichord stool.)

CONTE
Ehi...fammi lume.
Dove sarà Rosina?

COUNT
Hey...Give me some light.
Where can Rosina be?

(Rosina enters from her room. Figaro holds up his lantern.)

FIGARO
Ora vedremo...

FIGARO
We shall see...

(They see Rosina.)

Eccola appunto!

There she is!

CONTE
Ah, mio tesoro!

COUNT
Oh, my treasure!

ROSINA *(respingendolo)*
Indietro, anima scellerata!
Io qui di mia stolta credulità
venni soltanto a riparar lo scorno,
a dimostrarti qual sono
e quale amante perdesti,
anima indegna e sconoscente!

ROSINA *(repulsing him)*
Stand off, wretch that you are!
I have come here to wipe out
the shame of my foolish credulity,
to show what I am,
and what love you have lost in me,
unworthy and ungrateful man!

CONTE
Io son di sasso!

COUNT
I am petrified!

FIGARO
Io non capisco niente.

FIGARO
I don't know what she is talking about.

CONTE
Ma per pietà...

COUNT
But have pity...

ROSINA
Taci. Fingesti amore
per vendermi alle voglie
di quel tuo vil Conte Almaviva...

ROSINA
Be still. You pretended to love me
in order to sacrifice me to the lust
of the wicked Count Almaviva...

CONTE
Al Conte! Ah, sei delusa!
Oh, me felice!
Adunque tu di verace amore
ami Lindor...rispondi...

COUNT
Of the Count? Ah, you are deceived!
Oh, what happiness!
So you love Lindoro
truly...answer me...

ROSINA
Ah, sì!...t'amai pur troppo!

ROSINA
Oh, yes!...I loved you too much!

CONTE
Ah! non è tempo di più celarsi, anima mia;
ravvisa colui che sì gran tempo seguì tue
tracce, che per
te sospira, che sua ti vuole.
Mirami, o mio tesoro,
Almaviva son io, non son Lindoro.

COUNT
Oh, I shall keep it secret no longer, my
love; you see in me
the one who followed you for so long, who
yearns for you, who wants you to be his.
Look at me, my love,
I am Almaviva, I am not Lindoro.

disc no. 2/track 20   *Ah, qual colpo inaspettato!* At last, the elopement. As the briskly pulsing
music suggests, the Count and Rosina could not be happier. Figaro echoes the
same joyous melody, patting himself on the back for the good deeds he has
done. Rosina sings an ardent new melody **(02:57)**, which the Count takes up,
while Figaro, all but rolling his eyes impatiently, argues for haste in getting away.
Figaro sees someone, and he finally convinces the smitten lovers to get on—
quietly, very quietly—with the business of making a getaway **(04:52)**.

ROSINA
(Ah, qual colpo inaspettato!
Egli stesso? Oh Ciel! Che sento!
Di sorpresa e di contento
son vicina a delirar!)

ROSINA
(Oh, what a shock!
It is he himself! Heavens, what do I hear?
With surprise and with joy
I am almost delirious!)

FIGARO
(Son rimasti senza fiato,
ora muoion di contento,
guarda, guarda il mio talento,
che bel colpo seppe far!)

FIGARO
(They are breathless with delight,
they are dying of content,
oh, how talented I am,
what a coup I brought about!)

CONTE
(Qual trionfo inaspettato!
Me felice! Oh, bel momento!
Ah, d'amore e di contento
son vicino a delirar!)

FIGARO
(Son rimasti senza fiato:
ora muoion dal contento.
Guarda, guarda, guarda,
guarda il mio talento,
che bel colpo seppe far!)

ROSINA
Mio Signor!...Ma...voi...ma...io...

CONTE
Ah, non più, ben mio,
il bel nome di mia sposa,
idol mio, t'attende già, sì.

ROSINA
Il bel nome di tua sposa!
Oh, qual gioia al cor mi dà!

CONTE
Sei contenta?

ROSINA
Ah! mio signore!

ROSINA E CONTE
Dolce nodo avventurato
che fai paghi i miei desiri!
Alla fin de' miei martiri
tu sentisti, amor, pietà.

COUNT
(What triumph unexpected!
What a happy, wonderful moment!
With love and contentment
I am almost delirious!)

FIGARO
(They are breathless with delight,
they are dying of content.
Watch out, watch out, watch out,
how talented I am,
what a coup I brought about!)

ROSINA
My Lord!...But...you...but I...

COUNT
You are no longer just my love,
the blessed name of wife,
adored one, awaits you.

ROSINA
The blessed name of wife!
Oh, what joy that gives my heart!

COUNT
Are you happy?

ROSINA
Oh! Good sir!

ROSINA AND COUNT
Sweet, fortunate knot,
the end of all desire!
On our sufferings,
love, you took pity.

FIGARO
(Nodo!) Andiamo. (Nodo!)
Presto, andiamo. (Paghi!)
Vi sbrigate.
Lasciate quei sospir.
Presto, andiam per carità.
Ah, se si tarda, i miei raggiri
fanno fiasco in verità.
Ah! Cospetto! Che ho veduto!
Alla porta una lanterna, due persone!
Che si fa?

CONTE
Hai veduto...

FIGARO
Sì signor...

CONTE
Due persone?

(They run about in confusion.)

FIGARO
Sì signor...

CONTE
Una lanterna?

FIGARO
Alla porta, sì, signor.

ASSIEME
Che si fa? Che si fa?
Zitti, zitti, piano, piano,
non facciamo confusione,
per la scala del balcone,

FIGARO
(Knot!) Let's get going. (Knot!)
Quickly, Let's go. (All desire!)
Hurry up.
This is no time for sentiment.
Let's go quickly, for pity's sake.
Oh, if we delay my plans
will really come a cropper.
Oh, damnation! What do I see!
At the door a lantern, two persons!
What's to be done?

COUNT
You have seen...

FIGARO
Yes, sir...

COUNT
Two people?

FIGARO
Yes, sir...

COUNT
A lantern?

FIGARO
At the door, yes, sir.

TOGETHER
What's to be done?
Softly, softly, piano, piano,
no confusion, no delay,
by the ladder of the balcony,

presto andiamo via di qua.
Zitti, zitti, ecc.

quickly, let us go away.
Softly, softly, etc.

(Figaro leads them on to the balcony.)

FIGARO
Ah, disgraziati noi! Come si fa?

FIGARO
Oh, how unfortunate! What's to be done?

CONTE
Che avvenne mai?

COUNT
What happened?

FIGARO
La scala...

FIGARO
The ladder...

CONTE
Ebben?

COUNT
Well?

FIGARO
La scala non v'è più...

FIGARO
The ladder is gone...

CONTE
Che dici?

COUNT
What do you say?

FIGARO
Chi mai l'avrà levata?

FIGARO
Who could have taken it away?

CONTE
Qual inciampo crudel!

COUNT
What a cruel blow!

ROSINA
Me sventurata!

ROSINA
Oh, I am so miserable!

(They run into the corner; Figaro hides the lantern under his cloak.)

FIGARO
Zi...zitti! Sento gente...
ora ci siamo, signor mio.

FIGARO
Qu...quiet, I hear people...
And here we are, my master.

Che si fa?

CONTE
Mia Rosina, coraggio!

FIGARO
Eccoli qua.

(Basilio enters, followed by the notary.)

BASILIO
Don Bartolo...

FIGARO
Don Basilio...

CONTE
E quell'altro?

FIGARO
Ve' ve', il nostro Notaro.
Allegramente! Lasciate fare a me...

(He comes out of hiding and lifts the lantern high.)

Signor Notaro, dovevate in mia casa
stipular questa sera il contratto
di nozze fra il Conte d'Almaviva
e mia nipote. Gli sposi eccoli qua.
Avete indosso la scrittura? Benissimo.

BASILIO
Ma piano...Don Bartolo dov'è?

CONTE
Ehi! Don Basilio,

What's to be done?

COUNT
Courage, Rosina mine!

FIGARO
Here they are.

BASILIO
Don Bartolo...

FIGARO
Don Basilio...

COUNT
And who is the other?

FIGARO
Oh, oh, it's our notary.
How jolly! Leave it all to me...

Signor Notary, this evening in my house
you are to settle the contract
of marriage between the Count Almaviva
and my niece. Here is the couple.
Are the papers prepared? Very good.

BASILIO
But wait... where is Don Bartolo?

COUNT
Here, Don Basilio!

(Calling Don Basilio aside, he takes a ring from his finger and motions to him to be silent.)

quest'anello è per voi.

BASILIO
Ma io...

CONTE
Per voi vi sono ancor

(He plays with a loaded pistol under Basilio's nose.)

due palle nel cervello
se v'opponete...

BASILIO
Oibò! Prendo l'anello. Chi firma?

CONTE
Eccoci qua. Son testimoni
Figaro e Don Basilio.
Essa è mia sposa.

FIGARO
Evviva!

CONTE
Oh, mio contento!

ROSINA
Oh, sospirata mia felicità!

FIGARO
Evviva!

This ring is for you.

BASILIO
But I...

COUNT
For you two bullets in the head

are also waiting
if you offer any opposition...

BASILIO
Dear me! I'll take the ring. Who signs?

COUNT
Here we are. Figaro and
Don Basilio are witnesses.
This is my bride.

FIGARO
Evviva!

COUNT
Oh, how happy I am!

ROSINA
Oh, this is the joy I have longed for!

FIGARO
Evviva!

(Don Bartolo enters followed by an officer and soldiers. The townspeople press into the room after him.)

BARTOLO
Fermi tutti! Eccoli qua!

FIGARO
Colle buone, signor.

BARTOLO
Signor, son ladri,
arrestate, arrestate.

UFFICIALE
Mio signore, il suo nome?

CONTE
Il mio nome è quel d'un uomo d'onore.
Lo sposo io son di questa...

BARTOLO
Eh, andate al diavolo!
Rosina esser deve mia sposa: non è vero?

ROSINA
Io sua sposa?
Oh, nemmeno per pensiero.

BARTOLO
Come? Come, fraschetta?
Arrestate, vi dico,

(pointing to the Count)

è un ladro.

FIGARO
Or or l'accoppo.

BARTOLO
Halt, everyone! Here they are!

FIGARO
Gently, sir.

BARTOLO
Sir, they are thieves,
arrest them, arrest them.

OFFICER
Your name, sir?

COUNT
My name is that of a man of honour.
I am betrothed to this...

BARTOLO
Oh, go to the devil!
Rosina must be my bride: isn't that so?

ROSINA
I his bride?
Oh, I shouldn't dream of it.

BARTOLO
What? What's that, you hussy?
Arrest him, I tell you,

he's a thief.

FIGARO
I'll kill him on the spot.

BARTOLO
È un furfante, è un briccon.

UFFICIALE (al Conte)
Signore...

CONTE
Indietro!

UFFICIALE
Il nome?

CONTE
Indietro, dico, indietro...

UFFICIALE
Ehi, mio signor! Basso quel tono.
Chi è lei?

CONTE
Il Conte d'Almaviva io sono...

BARTOLO (rassegnato)
Insomma io ho tutti i torti...

FIGARO
Eh, purtroppo è così...

BARTOLO (a Basilio)
Ma tu, briccone, tu pur tradirmi
e far da testimonio!

BASILIO
Ah! Don Bartolo mio, quel signor Conte
certe ragioni ha in tasca,
certi argomenti a cui non si risponde.

BARTOLO
He's a knave, a rascal.

OFFICER (to the Count)
Sir...

COUNT
Stand back!

OFFICER
Your name?

COUNT
Back, I say, back!...

OFFICER
Now then, my dear Sir! Lower your voice.
Who are you?

COUNT
I am the Count Almaviva...

BARTOLO (resigned)
And I'm the one who's always wrong...

FIGARO
That's the way of things...

BARTOLO (to Basilio)
But you, you rascal, you too betrayed me
and acted as witness!

BASILIO
Ah! My good Doctor Bartolo, the Count
has certain reasons in his pocket,
and arguments to which there is no answer.

BARTOLO (*dichiarandosi vinto*)
Ed io, bestia solenne,
per meglio assicurare il matrimonio,
portai via la scala dal balcone!

FIGARO
Ecco che fa un' "Inutil precauzione"!

BARTOLO
Ma...e la dote?
Io non posso...

CONTE
Eh, via, di dote io bisogno non ho:
va - te la dono.

FIGARO
Ah! Ah! ridete adesso?
Bravissimo, Don Bartolo,
ho veduto alla fin rasserenarsi
quel vostro ceffo amaro e furibondo.
Eh! i bricconi han fortuna in questo mondo.

ROSINA
Dunque, signor Don Bartolo?

BARTOLO
Sì...sì...ho capito tutto.

CONTE
Ebben, dottore?

BARTOLO
Sì...sì...che serve?
Quel ch'è fatto è fatto.
Andate pur, che il ciel vi benedica.

BARTOLO (*accepting defeat*)
And I, stupid fool that I am,
the better to assure the marriage,
took away the ladder from the balcony!

FIGARO
Here is really the "Futile Precaution"!

BARTOLO
But...what about the dowry?
I cannot...

COUNT
Oh, come now, I do not need a dowry:
there...I present it to you.

FIGARO
Ha! Ha! You're laughing now?
Capital, Don Bartolo,
at last I've seen that bitter,
angry mug of yours brighten up.
Aha! Rogues are lucky in this world.

ROSINA
Well, Don Bartolo?

BARTOLO
Yes...yes...I understand perfectly.

COUNT
So...doctor?

BARTOLO
Yes...yes...what's the use?
What is done is done.
Go along with you, and may Heaven bless
 you.

FIGARO
Bravo, bravo, un abbraccio,
venite qua, dottore.

ROSINA
Ah, noi felici!

CONTE
Oh, fortunato amore!

FIGARO
Bravo, bravo, you deserve a hug,
come here, doctor.

ROSINA
Oh, happy us!

COUNT
Oh, fortunate love!

---

disc no. 2/track 23 *Di sì felice innesto* Figaro, the Count and Rosina each cheer the happy
turn of events, with the joyous encouragement of the chorus—another delightful
Rossini finale, with Rosina again piping her delight (01:52) over the ensemble.

FIGARO
Di sì felice innesto
serbiam memoria eterna.
Io smorzo la lanterna,
qui più non ho che far.

FIGARO
So happy a reunion
let us remember for ever.
I put out my lantern,
I am no longer needed.

(He blows out his lamp.)

**FIGARO, BARTOLO, BASILIO, CORO E
BERTA** *(che è entrata nel frattempo)*
Amor e fede eterna
si vegga in voi regnar.

**FIGARO, BARTOLO, BASILIO, CHORUS
AND BERTA** *(who has entered in the meantime)*
May love and faith eternal
reign in both your hearts.

ROSINA E CONTE
Amor e fede eterna
si vegga in noi regnar.

ROSINA AND COUNT
May love and faith eternal
reign in both our hearts.

ROSINA
Costò sospiri e pene
un sì felice istante:
alfin quest'alma amante
comincia a respirar.

ROSINA
We have hoped and sighed for
such a happy moment.
Finally this lover's soul
begins to breathe again.

TUTTI
Amore e fede eterna
si vegga in voi regnar.

CONTE
Dell'umile Lindoro
la fiamma a te fu accetta;
più bel destin t'aspetta;
su, vieni a giubilar.

TUTTI
Amore e fede eterna
si vegga in voi regnar.

FINE

ALL
May love and faith eternal
reign in both your hearts.

COUNT
You accepted humble
Lindoro's passion.
A brighter fate awaits you,
come then and rejoice.

ALL
May love and faith eternal
reign in both your hearts.

END

Translation C Capitol Records, 1952

Additional material translated by Gwyn Morris,

© 1975

The Barber of Seville

GIOACCHINO ROSSINI

COMPACT DISC ONE   76:56:00

1	Overture	7:26

Atto Primo/Act One

2	Piano, pianissimo, senza parlar *Fiorello/Coro/Conte*	2:57
3	Ecco ridente in cielo *Conte*	4:55
4	Ehi? Fiorello? *Conte/Fiorello/Coro*	1:06
5	Mille grazie, mio signore *Coro/Conte/Fiorello*	1:48
6	Gente indescreta! *Conte/Fiorello/Figaro*	1:13
7	La ran le ra la ran la la...Largo al factotum *Figaro*	4:33
8	Ah, che bella vita *Figaro/Conte*	2:17
9	Non è venuto ancora *Rosina/Conte/Bartolo/Figaro*	1:54
10	Le vostre assidue premure... *Figaro/Conte/Bartolo*	2:34
11	Se il mio nome saper voi bramate *Conte/Rosina/Figaro*	2:22

6	Ma vedi il mio destino!	0:52
	Bartolo	
7	Pace e gioia sia con voi	2:50
	Conte/Bartolo	
8	Insomma, mio signore, chi è lei?	2:22
	Bartolo/Conte	
9	Venite, signorine	1:04
	Rosina/Conte/Bartolo	
10	Contro un cor che accende amore	7:32
	Rosina/Conte	
11	Bella voce! Bravissima!	0:37
	Conte/Rosina/Bartolo	
12	Quando mi sei vicina	1:02
	Bartolo	
13	Bravo, signor barbiere, ma bravo!	2:52
	Bartolo/Rosina/Figaro/Conte	
14	Don Basilio!...Cosa veggio!	11:06
	Rosina/Conte/Figaro/Bartolo/Basilio	
15	Che vecchio sospettoso!	0:30
	Berta	
16	Il vecchiotto cerca moglie	3:27
	Berta	
17	Dunque voi Don Alonso	3:45
	Bartolo/Basilio/Rosina	
18	Storm	2:58
	Orchestra	
19	Alfine eccoco qua	1:36
	Figaro/Conte/Rosina	
20	Ah, qual cual colpo inaspettato!	6:18
	Figaro/Rosina/Conte	
21	Ah, disgraziati noi!	2:23
	Figaro/Conte/Rosina/Basilio/Bartolo/Uficiale	
22	Insomma io ho tutti i torti...	1:46
	Bartolo/Figaro/Conte/Rosina	
23	Di si felice innesto	2:16
	Figaro/Bartolo/Basilio/Berta/Coro/Rosina/Conte	